IS IT JUST MY CLOUD

A Novel Exploring Social Condition And Choice

MICHAEL J. CHARLES

Contact management @ blockcapitallist@gmail.com

ISBN: 9798741009680

Dedicated with sincere thanks to

Trevor Williams

Arts Educational School

Also, with great respect and honour to:

Edgar Allan Poe (1809-1849)

Fredrick Douglas (1818-1895)

Marcus Garvey (1887-1940)

Dr John Henrik Clarke (1915-1998)

Dr Yosef Ben-Jochannan (1918-2015)

Neely Fuller Jr (1929-2003)

Dr Frances Cress Welsing (1935-2016)

Dr Claud Anderson (www.powernomics.com)

And many more.....

CONTENTS

Introduction

CONFUSED? SIT BACK

I would like to tell you a story, a story about a cloud. You heard me right, I would like to tell you a story about a cloud, but I must say this is by far no ordinary cloud.

I beg of you to please hear me. I too feel your agitation and discomfort at the very thought of having to read a story about a cloud. But to this very end, I plead with you to have patience with me. So, in the interest of easing your ensuing discomforted state, I will take the liberty of describing to you the necessary details of this cloud.

I must also point out that on every occasion I have attempted to describe this cloud, I found myself pausing and almost taking on a trance-like state. An eerie silence overtakes the room, wherein what is only a matter of a few seconds feels much more like hours; its dense and ominous vapour seeping through the gaps in the window, and its presence looming ominously over my rooftop.

Oh! yes, sorry, I forgot myself, after all, I was meant to be describing to you this so-called non-ordinary cloud. Well picture this if you are so predisposed, this is a dense, massive, ghostly, stark, barren, cold and impetuous WHITE cloud.

I hear your gasps, and even some may find themselves choking at this description, but why is the question? Why indeed gasp? Why choke? At this point, I hear you say 'surely, he means it was an ugly, dense…', I must say I always get stuck when I try to think in the ways of others.

Anyway, needs must or is it must needs? Well, as I was saying, I hear you say, 'surely he means ugly, dense, wild, ghastly, dark and BLACK cloud?'. At this point, I fear this would be a good time to gather ourselves and reorganise our thoughts. The story of a cloud I would like to tell you is related to the former as opposed to the latter.

If then you can have patience with me, so that I can tell you the story about this cloud, then you may find that you too, in fact, are aware of it, and may even have great knowledge about it in your life. But I warn you, and I must warn you if I am to tell you a story about a cloud, I must first start right at the beginning. I ask of you only a few things, these things I fear are not too difficult, but under the circumstances, it will be easier for some than it will be for others. So then to the few little things, I ask of you:

1) Please locate a comfortable place to sit, lay or recline.

2) Please ensure that you have all snacks and goodies to hand, for your ease and comfort.

3) This element may prove to be more difficult than the former two, a little more difficult to achieve for some than for others. Please come with an open mind.

***

Chapter One

THE GIRL NEXT DOOR

IN the year Nineteen Hundred and Sixty-Six, an ordinary child was born in Paddington, London; in the spring, and to be a little more precise, in the month of March.

Well, as the case may be with so many of us, I do not have too many early memories but suffice to say it seemed normal, as far as I knew. By now it is August in the year Nineteen Hundred and Sixty-Nine, and our family, which comprised of my mother, two older sisters, and my eldest brother, moved into a brand new socially provided home.

I remember it so vividly; the street was buzzing with the excitement of the other families moving into the flats that were on the opposite side of the road to our brand-new house. At that point, I was already approaching my fourth birthday, and I can remember when we were allocated our rooms. My eldest brother and I had the smallest room, whilst my two sisters got the middle-sized room.

I also remember not being able to see out of the window without having to place both of my hands on the window ledge and pull myself up using both hands and feet. I am not sure if it was just in my mind, but back then it seemed like the summer was exactly that, summer; to that, I mean long periods of sunshine and days and weeks seemed to take an age to pass. I remember the great excitement in our house as each new day came with the discovery of new storage cupboards, or the skylight in the bathroom or the centrally heated system that was installed in the new buildings of that era.

I remember saying to myself, WOW! This place is so cool because it had pine wooden floorboards and the grubby old carpets that I used to crawl around on in the other house we lived in were, alas, no more. I must confess that it was at this point that, I learnt later on in life that the floorboards that I thought were such a great improvement from our last place were only visible because of poverty, as we could not afford to buy new carpets right away.

But by far, one of the greatest things about growing up in a working-class family such as ours was the great ability of our parents being able to create a world that was filled with love, care and compassion. I remember every day seemed to feel like it was my birthday or Christmas or some other kind of special occasion. I also remember playing outside and exploring this new street we had moved into. It was not a very busy street, in fact, it was a street that led into a main road to the east side and to the west side to a great big housing estate which I was to discover sometime later would become a very important place in my life.

I remember waking up on one Saturday or Sunday morning, and I really could not tell, as life was so blissful that I could not even tell one day from another. I woke up that morning having spent the night dreaming about exploring what was to be found at the back of our brand-new house. I could tell from the living room windows, which were set lower than the ones in the rooms upstairs, that at the back of the house it was very green; by green I mean lush green vegetation in the form of grass, trees, bushes and the sort.

That morning, I jumped out of bed and was very fortunate to have gotten to the bathroom before any of my sisters. I don't know if any of you have had the pleasure of living or growing up in a house with sisters but getting a chance to use the bathroom can only be described as no mean feat. Luck was on my side this glorious morning as I clipped the bathroom door behind me.

I set about sponging myself, as it was called by my mother in those days, I could hear her voice in my head saying, 'make sure you sponge yourself behind your ears, the back of your neck, under your arms and don't forget your Towley'. I know, I know, I hear you say to yourself 'what the hell is a Towley?'. Well, I will for now leave that to your imagination, though you will indeed soon discover the meaning of Towley in my story about a cloud.

My mother would even go as far as saying 'make sure you pull it back and wash underneath it too because you don't want any stale bread or cheese to be under there, just in case you get knocked down by a car, and they have to take you to the hospital'.

I guess at this point you may be in need of a more in-depth explanation of my escapades in the bathroom?

Well, as I have previously mentioned, coming from my particular background and indeed being working-class at this particular time, being clean was very important. I remember our parents saying, 'after you sponge yourself, make sure you put a clean set of underpants on'. This is where you were told it was just in case you came to some kind of misfortune of the kind previously mentioned, like getting knocked down by a car; or in my case, falling out of the tree I attempted to climb.

But I get ahead of myself, by now I have taken full advantage of the bathroom being free and I return to my room. I made sure I selected a clean pair of underpants and summarily put on the rest of my clothes. I remember walking out of the front door and walking to the top of the path. As I reached the top of the path, I noticed through my peripheral vision that there was a newcomer to our street. I must say that our eyes made contact right away and a truly pleasant exchange it was from my point of view.

Let me take the opportunity to describe her form as I saw it then, bearing in mind I didn't know that she was moving in with the rest of her family to a house just a few doors down from ours. She was, I think, what they called blond, she was slightly overweight for her age, but this only helped to make her more appealing to the eye. Her weight made her look as though she had started to form breasts, and her chubby size also meant that her buttocks would lift and raise her skirt with each and every step she took.

No sooner had our eyes met; a race of emotions came over me. She turned with a swish of her long blond hair and entered a gate at the top of her path and locked it behind her. I too turned as if to say I was not at all impressed with her either and made my way speedily to the plentiful orchard at the back of our house which ran the full length of our street. At length, I started to explore the many kinds of trees to be found. I remember counting in the small area that surrounded me with a selection of apple trees, pear trees, plum trees, cherry trees, and a few horse chestnut trees to boot.

By this time, I was fully engaged with my fantasies, creating small armies in my mind. I was a soldier caught behind the enemy line and had to call for full back up, 'Soldier one to soldier two.... over', 'Soldier one to soldier two.... over', Soldier two replies... 'reading you loud and clear, what is your exact position.... over', Soldier one replies, 'I'm pinned in from both flanks, and the main party of soldiers is coming straight towards my direction'.

At this point, deep in my fantasy of warfare, I suddenly had the feeling that eyes were on me. I did not look up right away for fear of realising that someone had been watching me mouthing off all parts of my imaginary war. I thought to myself, if I start humming, it may look as though I was humming all the time. 'La la la la la......' I could bear it no more, and so I felt compelled to lift my head.

To my great surprise, there waiting in the vision before me, was the slightly overweight blond girl from a few doors down from my house. She was perched on; I think it was the third step from the top. I must at this point confess to not knowing why I have retained this particular detail, but alas it was later to become a very important step in my life, that is of course if you may allow me this one little pun! It seemed that suddenly, the very idea of war, whether real or in my mind, had suddenly vanished.

Our eyes met followed by us both pretending to have something more interesting to do rather than look at each other. I summarily returned to my meaningless humming only to find my eyes compelled to look in her direction again. This time the glance was different from the first, this time I found my eyes lingered on her legs which were very visible due to the shortness of the little dress she was wearing. I remember seeing right up to her panty line, and remember a tingly feeling coming over me.

I beg your pardon and bid you to please remember me asking of you only a few things. I therefore appeal to you to have patience with me whilst I describe for you this feeling that came over me, that you may truly gain an understanding of my disposition at the time in question. The feeling which came about could be likened to an electronic pulse or the type of vibrating devices that your older sisters or parents had for the use of massage, we were told. I have heard that these vibrating devices now come in miniature or pocket-size applications, for instant and easy use.

As my mind had cleared from the thoughts of ruthless war games, I found myself walking in her direction. It was, to me, like I had been put into a trance-like-state ever beckoning towards her, by now her expression was different to that which she had expressed to me at the front of our houses. Now she had a very inviting expression, though I admit I am unable to express to you the exact composition of this inviting look.

I found myself at the foot of her steps. I stood there motionless for a moment with my head to the ground, and we both maintained a silence. It was at this point that I raised my head, ever-so-slowly at first then finished off with a final flick of the neck. It became very apparent to me that this girl wanted me to see what was to be found underneath her pretty short dress. Her legs were astride, and I remember the word PHAT! running across my mind. This, of course, was the work of my subconscious mind trying to explain and calculate the dimensions of this part of the body that I really did not have a name for. I bid therefore that you investigate your present life, time and space, and try to describe what is to be found at the top of a woman's thighs between her legs?

Suddenly, the feeling I had previously described to you came back, the electric pulse, the vibrating sensation and just an all-over feeling of exuberance came over me. I stared long and hard at this thing which I could not yet describe, the more I stared at it, the more it seemed her legs parted. The pulsating feeling continued, but this time it had an added dynamic feel to it, this time the pulse had transmitted to my Towley! My Towley, my Towley, it was as though it had taken on a complete life of its own.

I managed by now to lift my head to make full eye contact with her. I thought this would maybe help deal with this altogether new but highly pleasurable sensation that I had in the mid-region of my body. Well, I was completely wrong; on raising my head, all I was met with was a pair of big blue eyes and a warm smile. This only sought to confound my biggest fear at that moment, at that very moment, the pulses that had transmitted to my Towley were in full effect. My second biggest fear was that it would become visible to her and to all who may perchance make my acquaintance at that very moment.

To add to my already confused state, I was sure that my Towley was going to clean jump out of my trousers and climb the first two steps itself. It was akin to having a pet of some sort in your pocket, a strange thing to say, you may think to yourself, akin to having a pet in your pocket? Well, back in the Nineteen Hundred and Sixties, it was not thought of as being at all strange. In fact, there was much on TV that propagated such ideas, programmes such as Cat Weasel having a frog in his pocket for example, and much later Kez the Kestrel.

I finally regained some sort of mental control and attempted to introduce myself. 'My name is Michael', quickly she replied, 'my name is Jenny'. 'So, what are you doing?' I asked. She replied, 'nothing but you can sit next to me if you like'. She had not even finished what she was saying, and I jumped up the first two steps to sit right beside her. I could not help but notice that she had still not changed the orientation of her legs; in fact, they appeared to me to be getting even wider apart.

Tingle, tingle, tingle, is all I could feel as the same sensation continued its onslaught upon me. It seemed as if I couldn't contain it anymore, and as fast as the thought came to my mind, my right hand landed upon the inside of her left thigh. I tensed myself in the expectation of an adverse reaction, but lo! there was none. I remember making a fast brain calculation which said, 'if I turn my head to the opposite way to which she was facing, while at the same time move my right hand steadily up her thigh I might get to this bulge, this Pattie shaped thing to see what it felt like'.

I commenced with my brain calculated thought and received no adverse reaction, in fact, I received the complete opposite, a broad smile and what can only be described as a sigh of relief at what was taking place. My right hand explored some more and was able to make out that it was a spongy type of thing, with three rather distinctive parts. These comprised of two burger bun type elements, coupled with a space in the middle that the burger would normally occupy.

My hands, as if on automatic pilot, managed to slither their way down into the panty line, my middle finger seemed to naturally find its direction once inside. The two burger-like parts parted and appeared to become swollen and ever so slightly moist. Suddenly a noise filled the air! It was the sound of my mother's voice alerting me to the fact that it was time to come in for lunch. We both froze for a moment, then all in one swift movement, I retrieved my hand and bade my new friend goodbye and skipped off in a perfect state of alacrity. Just as the voice was about to repeat Michael! I replied, 'yes mum', with a smile transfixed across my face, mum asked 'why do you have such a big smile on your face?'. With a confidence that belied my age, I replied, 'I am smiling because I am happy to see your face'.

I remember that meal being despatched in a flash, the whole time I had been going over the entire events of that morning in my head. I vaguely remember my mother's voice saying something like 'slow down boy you will do yourself damage', I continued head on until the last bite. At the end of that meal, I remember my mother saying to me, make sure your food has been fully digested before you go back outside to play.

Though it was perfect weather to go back out into the open air, for some strange and yet compelling reason, I did not want to venture back outside. Instead, I had an irresistible urge to go upstairs and lay down and contemplate the morning's events. I confess to having left out a minor detail that also led to the decision to stay in on this most beautiful summer day. Alas, the confession related to my old friend Towley. Towley had been as stiff as a board throughout lunch, and in truth, it felt as if it would never abate.

At length, I attempted to retire to my room, but each time I attempted to move, Towley was still present and undisguisable, but I eventually managed to make good my escape and retire to the fragile privacy of my bedroom. There I lay and drifted off into thought. I lay on my back and looked up at the ceiling and lo! just below the ceiling was a small fluffy white cloud.

***

Chapter Two

THE ADVENTURE PLAYGROUND

B Y now a few years have passed, and I seem to have regular visits from this fluffy white cloud. In fact, I noticed this cloud was not unique to me. As I mentioned in my earlier chapter, there was a housing estate to the west side of my street; this estate was a hub of excitement that never seemed to sleep.

I noticed that this cloud crossed the racial divide, and it was clear that all sections of the community had them, but with some subtle differences. I could not help but notice that, although the clouds crossed the racial divide, the differences were much more noticeable with the older people. By older, I mean the groups that consisted of teenagers and above; an age range of about fourteen to twenty-four years of age.

Though the vast majority of the people I would see had fluffy white clouds floating above them, some seemed to be gleaming while others seemed to be fading, and in some cases, some dribbled a pus-like entity. I wondered at length what could be making those clouds behave and look so different, I would often check the status of my little white cloud and found it to be more on the gleaming side.

Though a few years had passed since my affair on the back steps of my neighbour's house, I feel compelled to confess that I had, on many occasions, similar titillations to this point. A funny thing I noticed along this journey is that on each occasion, it seemed to me that all my encounters had been with girls from the same racial group. This by itself was not in any way at all unusual, but the effects therefrom, I must say was for me, a major bone of contention later on.

But before I relate to you this bone of contention, I must first relate to you a story of just one of these girls. Her name was Katy, and I tell you this, she was by no means an ordinary ten year old girl. Katy belied her age and could set the whole estate on alert if she had been seen out. This day then related to us being in the adventure playground, which was situated directly behind my house. The usual crew were present and accounted for, which consisted of Hooly, Fod, Spaceman, Pricey to name but a few.

As if out of nowhere, a voice came steaming into the park panting for breath. Fod came running in shouting 'quick, quick!' he exclaimed. 'Katy is out and she's coming to the adventure playground!'. It seemed that all at once everybody jumped into the air, rather like a flock of startled birds, and on landing, it seemed almost synchronised, in a mad panic to tidy our clothes. For one thing, Katy never had a permanent suitor; she would always pick someone new on the spot. This, of course, meant that we were all in with an equal shot, although it would always help if you had been lucky enough to have been blessed with a new pair of training shoes, or some other item worthy of discussion.

Panic over and the atmosphere calmed down, with each of us momentarily entering our own mind hoping and wishing that we may be the object of her desires. This moment seemed to last forever and was only broken by a whisper from one of us. I confess to not remembering this minor detail, as to which one of us that was, in view of the prevailing circumstances, but with a swish of her hair, Katy entered the park, and her presence filled the park with an air of excitement and adventure. She made her way purposefully towards the swings. Hooly, Spaceman, Pricey, Fod and I followed en-suite. She arrived at the swings and proceeded to sit on one; the games had just begun!

At this point, Katy had not even given us the slightest of glances in our direction, and the ensemble that we made up had arrived in the playground just in front of the swings. Katy had chosen her swing well, as this particular one was situated in the middle of the range of swings, which meant that there was a panoramic view of her at all times and more importantly any of the actions she might make.

Katy started as she meant to go on, on this occasion, she had still not given us a single glance but no sooner had we gathered our thoughts, Katy prised her legs wide apart. Now as I have said, this is a few years after my first encounter with my neighbour on her back steps, by now we all knew exactly what was being shown, the dilemma was which one of us, if any, will she choose to share it with.

As young boys of the age range of ten to thirteen years old, the sight of such a wonderful gift was not to be ignored. The sight of a furry burger that was just sprouting the evidence of puberty became immediately apparent that we were all having major interactions with our Towleys - here is that word again and I safely assume that you have grasped its full meaning at this point in my story about a cloud?

Katy continued her tease, and we became more and more excited at the prospect of the possibility that one of us will be able to feel its youthful pleasures before the day was out. For the very first time since Katy arrived in the adventure playground, she looked in our direction. As if by magic we all stood erect and to attention, with each one saying in their minds 'please pick me, please pick me', shortly followed by the thought 'you slut if she does not pick me'. It was true irony in play, and we played boisterous games in a bid to impress her and gain her favour.

May I take this opportunity to explain a few things that I feel are pertinent at this point. One is that Katy was no ordinary ten year old girl; she possessed an air of superiority and had a TV or stage-like presence to her. The second thing was that, although we used the phrase slut, we did not have any idea of what it actually meant, suffice to say we were still very much in the race to see who would be so fortunate to revel in its pleasures.

By chance or fate, I was lucky enough to have been given a brand new pair of monkey boots that morning. I confess to them not being Dr Martins, which were the rage of the day, but monkey boots were the poor man's version, and lo and behold, I had them on! Katy looked at all of us in turn, inspecting us from head to toe, each one of us and maybe holding her glance if she found something of interest. Lucky for me, on this occasion, Katy exclaimed 'those are nice boots, nice and shiny and bright!'

My heart raced, and I confess to having a moment of self-induced suffocation, or some other similar affliction. I responded as any so-called cool ten year old boy would, 'yeah they're alright', to this I expected a hostile response, but to my utter amazement, it seemed to be exactly what she wanted to hear. By using her hands, she put pressure on the swing and eased her buttocks gently off the swing. She walked slowly towards me and proceeded to run her fingers down my chest. She then turned away and walked to the slide where she took up position by laying on her back, looking up at the bright blue sky. As I have already mentioned, she had a TV or stage-like presence that belied her age. She, as if compelled, started to roll and gyrate her hips, this to all of us was a sight to behold; we turned in her direction, which only helped to increase her enthusiasm. She bumped and rolled and gyrated her hips even more vigorously, and while that was happening, we were all becoming more and more transfixed on her shape and form.

'Pick me, pick me, please pick me', was the only thought running through all our minds. Katy continued the assault on our frail and ill-formed sexual minds, we all stepped over to the slide and what could only be described as an encircled sensual vision. Katy enquired 'which one of you wants to come and lay on top of me?'. It feels much better when you can feel the heat and the motion of somebody else. We all said in unison 'me, me, me', we jostled somewhat for a moment, one against the other. Suddenly she called out and as if by strange and unexplained reason, I could no longer comprehend English for a moment.

Suddenly I was able to make out through my utter dismay and excitement, that she had said my name. I hardly gave her a second chance to change her mind, so I adjusted my Towley to make sure it would have full effect once it was pressed against her pelvic bone. I, as I have previously mentioned, had many great occasions where I have been able to exercise my pelvic prowess, and I intended this moment to be no exception to that rule.

I climbed on top tentatively at first, but no sooner had I felt the bulge she had between her legs I could scarcely control myself. I pumped and pounded like my life depended on it. I must at this time point out that there was a rule that if you were ever lucky enough to be picked, the rule was very simple in that it was said, the ones who were not lucky on any occasion could stand and watch the opening build-up, but then they must leave without making a scene or interrupt the proceedings.

With this in mind, I must say, it allowed me to pull off a fantastic performance. Katy seemed to appreciate my enthusiasm and directed me to her not so formed breasts, but it was never really about her breasts. Katy was known much more for her southernly movements; she surely knew how to move those hips! And coming from that particular racial group, it seemed to me to be even more exciting. Anyway, I see myself leaving the point for which I do sincerely apologise, but by now the lads knew their roles at this point, and I was able to lift my head momentarily and glimpse the back of them as they walked out of the adventure playground.

It seemed clear to me by this point that I would not suffer the Black Widow Tale. The tale went thus in short, if Katy suddenly changed her mind, she could quite easily call out to one of your counterparts to take your place. It seemed then that on this very occasion, I was the true desire, she intensified the heat after doing the best I could with her barely formed breasts, she moved me straight in for the kill. As if in a single move, my hand was nestled in the warm pelvic area, as she continued to tantalise with ever more vigour and lo! the feeling of a wet sensation took over my fingers. I knew by this time very well what that sprouting pubic hair moisture was, as you may remember in my earlier encounter with my neighbour on her back-door step in those days, we used to call it a fur burger. Now that we were more grown, we referred to that particular part of the anatomy as the Catty; I need not, I hope, go into any great speech about why it is named as such. I slipped my hand to and fro between her ever-swelling Catty and to my utter joy, it was responding a treat, evermore wet, evermore swollen. I admit this is the furthest that I had ever gotten than on previous encounters. Suddenly my middle finger was pushed deep into her evermore moist region.

My entire body responded to the electrifying feeling that her movement and utter confidence had commanded. I continued to thrust my pelvis even more rapidly this time against her leg, all the while I continued to push my middle finger ever deeper into her inviting warm abyss. This continued for some time, all the while the sexual tension was rising more and more.

It seemed, for a moment, that Katy stopped and looked at me, she gave me a look that could only be described as one which says, I want all that you would care to give me. We both simultaneously looked around the park to see if we were alone. It was obvious, at once that we were totally alone. We looked back at each other, and as if with an unspoken language, we started to expose our genitals. This was a first.

My heart pounded rapidly as the excitement had reached fever pitch, Ah! At once, we both sighed as our naked parts met. Instant ecstasy, my Towley was as stiff as any respected cricketers' bat. I must also point out that by this time, I knew well that I was the carrier of a secret weapon. As Freud had said, many of our sexual encounters happen in or around the home, to that then my case was no exception. My dear cousin, Gillian had mentioned that for my age, I was very well endowed, so I always had an air of confidence that said, if I was lucky enough to be chosen and get past the first round, I would certainly be best placed to please.

So it seemed that for an age, we set about pumping and grinding each movement giving out more pleasure than the one before it. Katy looked like she did not have a single care in the world. I too, therefore, took my role very seriously and stroked my stiff Towley rapidly in and out of her wet Catty lips. I could scarcely contain myself, as I could feel an intense sensation particularly around the head of my Towley as I, at length, reckoned in my mind this utterly amazing feeling.

The feeling only seemed to have one intention, and that was to cause some kind of incendiary bang. I wondered again at length whether this is the thing older guys talk about up at the cricket nets, which incidentally is the smokers' corner or at least it was in our school. I noticed on each downward thrust that my Towley would get an increased shock-like feeling, again in my head I said to myself 'could this be the entrance to the chamber the older boys also talked about?'. Suffice to say in both cases, I really did not know the answer, but Katy seemed to be at total ease and made it clear that this was to be the mode of the day.

At length we continued to pound one another to great effect, now it would seem we were both getting the same shocks and at the same time. Katy said to me, 'can you feel that?' I replied, 'can I feel what?'. An awful silence came about, and for a moment, I had thought it was all totally blown now. Again, luck favoured me very much on this day, she sighed and got right back to moving her well-tuned pelvic area.

You would not be wrong in thinking this is all happening in a public place, and yes you would be right. But as aforementioned, luck was very much on my side that day, we both struggled to contain the feeling, and I had finally found the right words to say. I exclaimed, 'do you mean this feeling?' and I added 'I mean when my Towley touches this part with the hole?'. To my utter amazement again she said 'exactly, have you ever put it in?'. I nearly, for the second time, said a ridiculous comment, but again luck had it that I was able to give a direct response.

Sadly 'no' I retorted and waited to see if she would make fun of me for that very fact, but no, she said in the sexiest voice 'would you like to?'. I stuttered and said, 'very much so'. Katy, in her ever so cool persona, said, 'well go on then'. My mind seemed to be running in all directions, my heart was beating ten to the dozen. I grabbed my Towley tight and embarked on a new adventure, all the time we are both dripping wet as our sexual organs had found a new gear. I confess this then could be my big chance to go up to the cricket nets and stand face to face with the older boys and relate to them my truth.

As I tried to grip my Towley evermore, I notice a trembling in my hand, Oh no! Not the nerves and shakes again. This was also a major topic with the older guys, but this always seemed to be used as a tool for laughing at someone. It was often said that 'so and so burst in a second', or 'so and so burst on contact', bear with me a moment's patience I have afore told you about how sensational the feeling was as we pumped each other. Still, now there had been an added dynamic, she now needed me to act like one of the big guys and really do it.

I am not sure why, at this particular moment, my mind went on to my little fluffy white cloud, strange you might think, but in truth, it was not at all strange. I looked at my cloud and it appeared to me to be getting a little larger and even brighter, I could not understand why on each encounter of this nature my cloud would become larger and increase its brilliance in colour.

Katy beckoned again 'come on stick it in'. In an attempt to disguise my utter fear, nerves, and excitement, I suggested that we pumped a little more. To this, I think she more reluctantly said ok, I made all the best moves I could think of, the moves us guys would practice behind the garages that ran along the River Brent. Let me make it clear at this very early point that we did not practice on each other in any way. Moreover, we used to direct each other's movements and style.

I said to myself, you can no longer run away from this, however nice I might have thought the feelings of just pumping were, on this occasion I was going to have to do more. Again, I took on a stiff grip of my still stiff and moist Towley and set about trying to push it inside of her. My hands started to tremble yet again, but there was nothing to be done this time, I pushed and again I pushed, and on each occasion, it was obvious that it would not go in. Katy paused for a moment also as if to say, 'let me do it', she then took hold of my Towley, and I must say she squeezed it with the right tension.

She attempted no less than twice but still no joy, everything was moist, the Towley was hard as a cricketer's bat but still, it would not enter. I could feel the mood changing rapidly and thought is there any way this wonderful afternoon could be saved. Katy tried several more attempts, but she could not get it to enter, the mood sunk evermore, and I wished I knew the reason my moist Towley could not enter this so inviting Catty. No sooner had I tried to give it some thought, Katy whispers in my ear that someone was coming into the park to walk their dog. In truth as much as I was disappointed this encounter was over, a sense of relief overtook me as well, and as children do, we systematically tried to pull our clothes back in order as if to assume older people had no idea what we were doing.

As we managed to put our dishevelled personages back in one piece, we started to make our way out of the adventure playground, all the while Katy and I walked in complete silence. I looked up at the cloud above Katy's head and noticed that some of her cloud was leaving her and it seemed to be joining mine. Is this how all these strange clouds form? I had up until this point never noticed this transference before, though I was certain that after each encounter of this nature there would always be a change to my fluffy white cloud, this day then was to be no exception.

Katy and I continued up the path of the adventure playground, as we reached the top of the path where the gate was situated, I needed to turn right and Katy to the left. We continued to walk out of the park in complete silence. If Katy's silence was for the same reason as mine, then I would expect her to have a warm feeling from within and a still slightly over-expressive pulse rate. I also wondered if Katy could see my cloud or even her own for that matter, I very rarely saw people from her racial group ever look at their clouds, it was as if they never even knew they were there.

We finally exited the park and Katy turned to me and said, 'I had a really good time today' to my utter surprise and apparent amazement I replied by saying, 'the same here'. Before we went on our separate ways, Katy also enquired if we could, maybe do the same again? On this occasion there was no hesitation in my reply, 'make it as soon as you can' I said, and to my pretty smart reply, I was given the warmest of smiles to send me on my merry little way.

I walked from around the back of my house to the front, where I noticed two older guys standing there and they were from the same racial group as me. I could not help but notice how very large their clouds were, and the fact that they had become very, very, discoloured. I could scarcely keep myself from staring at these two guys, I noticed that they were in deep discourse and that it seemed rather fiery. I took a moment to have a look at my fluffy white cloud. Again, my cloud seemed to become even brighter and fluffier than the day before.

The two guys continued their way in the westerly direction of our street. I regained my conscious thoughts again and made my way down the path to my house. I got in and went straight upstairs, like many years past, I lay on my bed and looked up at the ceiling and started to contemplate the very exciting events of the day. I thought of the guys who were not as fortunate as I was on this day, Hooly, Pricey, Spaceman and Fod. I confess that this was only for the briefest of moments but nonetheless a thought.

I continued to lay on my back and pondered on what these clouds could be, and whether we could all see them? I asked myself, why are they so different and what is the reason for the difference? I must have pondered until I fell asleep, I was awakened by the sound of my sister's voice calling out to me, 'Michael! Hooly and Fod have come over to see you'. I jumped off the bed and rubbed my eyes and made my way downstairs.

***

Chapter Three

ATTACK BY THE RIVER BRENT

A S I got down to the final step, I sat down to tie the laces of my monkey boots. Once my laces were tied, I ran into the kitchen and went to the freezer for one of my mother's homemade blackberry ice lollies. The amazing thing about these ice lollies was that they were 100% organic, all the blackberries therein were picked, ironically, from the adventure playground situated at the back of my house. My mother was famously known on our street for making amazing cakes and organic ice lollies.

I reached into the freezer and pulled out three ice lollies. The guys were made up and off we set up the path. As we all started to lick our ice lollies, it was evident that the guys wanted to know how my eventful encounter had ended. I admit to feeling rather smug at this point and in a rather stern voice told the guys 'remember not to throw away my mum's plastic lolly sticks'. The guys retorted simultaneously 'Michael, we know! This is not the first time we have had the pleasure of one of your mother's delicious lollies, so, come on then, what happened, what happened?'. It was as if there was an echo effect permeating from Hooly and Fod.

We made our way towards the easterly direction of my street. About twenty metres away from my house was a little church that, as far as we could tell, was owned by Americans. The church was, for the most part, never really used, but every couple of summers our street would be full of children from the U.S.A, and there was always an air of excitement whenever they came. Alas then, this was not one of these occasions, we made our way to this little church and sat on the wall that encircled it.

We all picked our spot on the wall and sat down. We were sitting in silence at this point, which was mainly due to the sheer taste of our organic blackberry ice lollies. At length, the silence was finally broken by Hooly who exclaimed, 'I can't take it anymore, tell me, I beg you, tell me what happened in the adventure today!'. I paused as I took a big slurp of my ice lolly, I turned my head in the direction of both Fod, and Hooly and raised one eyebrow as if to say, 'wouldn't you like to know'. I leave it to your imagination the barrage of superlatives that were thrown in my direction, in truth they bounced off me like I had employed the help of a Kevlar vest, I slurped on my ice lolly once more and began my oratory.

I scarcely started my oratory when I noticed a twitching happening in the groin area of Fod's trousers, 'Fod! Man! I haven't even started to get to it yet and you standing already?' 'Mate I am not sure I want to continue', I said. I got a thump from both Hooly and Fod, 'come on tell us what happened man, all we know those kinds of pumps you were putting down there was nothing to be sniffed at'. Fod exclaimed 'what do you think gave me this stiffy then? It was the memory of you on top and her underneath you giving as good as she was getting'. I continued my account of the afternoon when suddenly we heard loud voices, they seemed to be coming from the east side of my street the very part that led to the main road.

Before long, the voices had become even louder, and we could suddenly see the people who were making the noise. It was a very large group of guys that consisted of people wearing green bomber jackets, tight jeans with turn-ups and high laced boots with steel toe caps. Suddenly the events of the day had lost its lustre because it became evident that there was somebody in the centre of this group looking incredibly frightened and scared. We heard this person pleading to be left alone, but every time he asked for mercy, he was either punched or kicked. We all looked at each other as if to search for the meaning of what we were witnessing, our gaze came right back to its starting position, and we all seemed even more perplexed.

The large group of teenage boys continued past the little church down my road, which led to the River Brent. All the while we could hear the wailing and howling of this very poor person in the centre of the group. We asked each other who were these people, as we had never seen a group of this nature before, and more importantly, not in our neighbourhood. We, young ten to thirteen year olds, followed this group behind the church and on to the river. The large group of boys led the way into the deep bushes, which also led to the dark tunnel that led to the bread factory on the other side.

The group got to a part of the river where the banks were very much higher than the water levels. At this point, there was a massive tree that had been fixed with a rope the older guys had used to swing across the river. I have had many fun days watching the older guys swinging across the river and picking someone up from the opposite bank, then transferring them to the other side.

Today, alas, was not one of those fun days, this day had a much graver outlook attached to it. The group of guys had cans of beer or lager in their hands and would sip on them and laugh and cheer out loudly, all the while this boy at the centre of the group kept on pleading to be let free. Hooly, Fod and I noticed that there was also one guy that stood out from all the others with the same green bomber jackets, and boots, this guy was massive, that was the only way to describe him.

He shared the same racial group as me, Hooly and Fod, but did not share the same racial group as the other guys he was with. This large guy seemed to have a leading role in what was happening. He was often consulted whenever somebody wanted to kick or punch the young guy they surrounded; on most occasions, he would give the nod, and some kind of pain would be inflicted on this poor young guy.

I paused for a moment and went into my own mind, trying to make sense of what we were witnessing. I then opened my eyes and looked at the clouds above all their heads. There was a mass of white clouds and in some cases, it looked like they had merged into each other to make a super cloud. There was the cloud of those who shared the same racial group, but the thing that struck me as being most odd was the fact that the leader of this group, who happened to come from the same racial group as us, had no other cloud merging with his.

The leader had a cloud, yes, and it was white fluffy and very, very large, but strangely enough, it never merged with the mass of the group. The leader sat on high to find a great vantage point from which he could survey the proceedings. The group that made up the largest number looked again towards the leader for the grand command to carry out what they had come there to do. The leader raised his hand then dropped it like he was the starting official of a race, the group of guys became frenzied with excitement, jumped about and started to shout very nasty things to the poor guy in the centre of the group.

One shouted 'get on your fucking knees you lackey bastard, on your fucking knees', to this there was a mighty cheer. The little guy slumped to his knees and the group set on him punching and kicking. This, by now, had been going on for about ten to fifteen minutes or so, the very same cry, 'say you're a fucking lackey', and the little guy would reply by saying 'I am not a lackey, I am just a guy'. Smash! As the sound of the steel toe-capped boots landed in the centre of his face. Hooly, Fod and I could scarcely watch, but it was also hard to tear ourselves away, it was like the Imp of the Perverse, you know the outcome but are unable to stop yourself from exploring it anyway.

The blows kept on raining in the whole time as we saw the little guy being knocked from pillar to post. He would be knocked down and then he would stand up on his knees, only for someone to come running in and knock him back down to the ground again. He again pleaded to be released, but it was to no avail, the group had become even more inflamed and more and more frenzied. The group beckoned to the leader of the group to come down and finish him off; the group cheered and chanted 'Bruiser, Bruiser, Bruiser!' All the while, the leader of the group flexed his muscles and continued to bask in his glory. One more crash and a thud of a punch and a kick, down again he went, each time he got weaker and weaker but, on every occasion, he just popped back up.

By now the little guy in the middle was on his knees and had major cuts and bruises, he pleaded and pleaded with the group to let him go and repeated the fact that he was not a lackey but just a guy. This seemed to inflame the group even more so, as they cheered at each one of his pleas, the blood steadily pouring from what would seem to be every conceivable orifice. The blood would spray out each time he was punched or kicked again, the leader finally took to his feet and with a roar likened to a Roman gladiator arena the group of guys once again cheered 'Bruiser, Bruiser, Bruiser!'.

The massively built leader made his way down the bank to the little guy, who seemed barely alive at this point. The leader walked over to him and took him by his hair and lifted his head slowly. He then proceeded to punch the little guy, who was still on his knees, several times in the face. With each blow, large splatters of blood would spray out in all directions. The little guy was wailing and screaming for mercy, but mercy was nowhere to be found at this time. The leader kept up the raining blows as the little guy flopped and buckled up under pressure. 'Please, please, please' he begged, and the more he begged, the more he would feel the wrath of their convictions. I was sure this little guy was dead or, if not, very close to it. The rest of the group were silent and fully engaged with the performance.

The blood was still pouring out of this little guy. By now it was obvious that the three of us were frozen to the spot and any attempt to leave would arouse suspicion that we would be calling for help. The leader pushed his strong arms into the air and punched as if to punch the sky, 'Bruiser, Bruiser, Bruiser' they continued to chant. It was clear that an end was about to come to the earth-shattering and ghastly experience. The leader walked around the little guy as if he was prey that had been captured and was being used as a play toy. He paced around his victim and with a sudden movement, kicked the little guy square in the face.

This time the blood sprayed out in every conceivable direction. The little guy let out the loudest yelp and cry I had ever heard and, hopefully, was ever likely to hear again. The little guy slumped to the ground and lay there motionless. The group came back to life, and the shouting and cheering continued to fill the air. The whole time the little guy lay motionless on the ground. My heart felt empty. I turned and looked at Hooly and Fod, and I noticed a tear in their eyes. I must confess at this time that there was more than a single tear in my eye, I knew this would be something I would never forget. Just as we thought it might all be over new chants began, 'chuck him in, chuck him in, chuck him in' rang out from the entire group. A few members of the larger group made their way back down the bank to where this motionless body lay; two guys grabbed the legs and another two grabbed his arms.

The guys lifted the lifeless and motionless body and started to swing him as if he was a skipping rope. They swung him back and forth, building up even more momentum on each swing. After three they said, 'One, Two, Three' and with a mighty swing they threw the little guy into the deepest part of the river. He landed, and there was no movement to be seen, the guys cheered and spat and pissed in the water where they had just thrown him in. The command was issued 'let's go!'. The leader had sounded an end to the ordeal, all the while our hearts were beating ten to the dozen, we could, it would seem, not even speak much less think.

The leader led the group back through the thick bush in the direction of the small church on my road—the whole time they sang and joked about what had just happened. Hooly, Fod and I followed the group back to the street, and we made sure we kept a safe distance because we could not be sure these guys would not turn on us. Now that I was regaining my ability to think, I thought at length as we walked back to the road. I wondered who these people were? I had never seen the likes of them before, and fear came upon me that this could happen to any one of us, there did not seem to be anything to suggest that this was not the case.

Finally, the group reached the back of the church and continued in an easterly direction back to the main road. The whole time they kept on with the singing and cheering as they went on. Fod could hardly contain it anymore, Fod exclaimed 'what the fuck was that?'. Hooly and I remained silent. I guess this was due to us not knowing exactly what we had just witnessed. The three of us made our way back to the front of the church and reclaimed the spots we had found on the wall before the whole encounter had begun. We sat in complete silence all the while searching and wondering what we had just witnessed. Fod again said 'guys what the hell did we just see', I replied by saying 'I haven't a clue, but I am sure we may have just witnessed somebody being killed'. This, as I imagine you might think, brought about an even bigger silence, 'what if he is?' I said. Hooly and Fod both said, 'no he is not dead'. I thought to myself, how can they be so sure because I felt certain that the little guy was no more.

As we sat in silence, I could not help but recount in my mind what I had just witnessed, the image of this little guy pleading for mercy. On each occasion he pleaded, he was set upon, even more. I could scarcely remove the image of the blood splattering in all directions and being kicked in the face by the steel toe-capped wearing gang. I was also very concerned to know what name such a group would be known as, so I asked my two companions for suggestions, but none of us knew who they were.

By now the sun was going down and it was time for us to make our way back home. For me, luckily, my house was just beside the little church, and this meant there was not too much walking for me to do. This also meant that I did not have to face the chance of meeting that very dangerous group again, which was, alas, not the case for both Hooly and Fod. We bid each other goodbye and set upon our separate way, and after a short walk, I arrived home. I knocked on the door in an urgent manner and as soon as the door was opened, I rushed in and asked for my older brother. I was told he was in the bathroom,

I thought to myself what a truly inconvenient time to have a need for the bathroom.

I ran upstairs to the room I shared with my older brother and waited until he came out. I was sure that was his first stop to dress for whatever occasion he was inconsiderably invited to on this very day of my emotionally challenged self. What I expected was nothing more than five or so minutes, but it seemed to take a lifetime. 'Come on, come on, what could he possibly be doing in there all this time?' I said. I heard the lock of the bathroom door unclip, at last, I thought, he was on his way.

No sooner had my brother exited the bathroom, I came running out of the bedroom and pounced on him. 'Paul', I said 'I have just witnessed the most awful thing'. Paul said, 'relax and take a deep breath then tell me what happened'. 'There were loads of them all in green jackets and big boots'. Paul said, 'who was in green jackets?'. Like I said, 'there were loads and loads of them, I'm certain they killed him'. It was at this point my brother sat me down and said, 'now start from the top, now what did you see?'. 'Paul, there were loads of boys, they seemed to have a uniform on'.

The uniform consisted of a GREEN BOMBER JACKET, LARGE STEEL TOE-CAPPED BOOTS, TIGHT JEANS WITH TURN UPS AND HAIR CUT SHORT. At that point, I noticed a strange look overtake my brother. Besides my mother, my brother was, to me, the most powerful person in the whole universe. To witness the look on his face immediately indicated that there was something to be concerned about. He beckoned me to continue with my account all the while my brother was still only wearing a towel around his waist.

My brother sat on the other end of the bed to await my full account. 'Well, Fod, Hooly and I were sitting on the wall of the church beside the house, we were slurping on one of mum's organic ice lollies, when suddenly....' I went into the full account of what we had just witnessed. It was at this point that I noticed my brother's cloud in a way I had never noticed it before. My brother's cloud was very much like that of the two boys that shared the same racial group as my brother and I, but his cloud was not white and fluffy like mine.

My brother's cloud was much larger and discoloured, it was silken black. I use the phrase discoloured because I measured his against my fluffy white cloud. I later discovered that this was not the best way to describe his cloud, and that of the two guys I had seen in the past at the front of the house. At great lengths, I tried to continue with my account of what I had seen 'he was being beaten kicked and all sorts, they had finally got him to where the big rope was where we used to swing across the river'. My brother knew the spot very well, so he beckoned me to continue, 'well they got him to the river bank and encircled him ever taunting and beating him'.

My brother asked, 'did they have a leader, this group of guys with the green bomber jackets?' 'Yes' I said at once, 'or at least it seemed like they had a leader'. My brother said, 'I shall describe this leader to you', I was to tell him if he was correct. All the time I still wanted to know who this group was, so without hesitation, I said, 'go ahead'. My brother described a tall character very muscular and fit, I with utter astonishment said 'yes! do you know who he is?'.

My brother paused and mumbled 'they are here now', I said 'who are here now?'. At this point, my brother finished getting dressed. He seemed to have a sense of urgency and was putting on the first things that came to hand, this I thought was strange because my brother always took great pride in his appearance. All the while I am badgering my brother, 'who is here now, who is here?'.

My brother continued to evade the question, and summarily put the rest of his clothes on. He seemed to move all in one swift movement and left the room and was downstairs, shouting to mum 'I am just going to Tennason's house' and with that, I heard the sound of the front door closing behind him and he was gone. I got off the bed and ran to the window to see which direction my brother would go in. He walked at great speed to the top of the path and turned in a westerly direction towards the side that leads to the estate at one end of my road.

I watched my brother walk down our street to as far as my eyes would let me, as he finally got out of sight I returned to the bed and sat down and pondered on the idea that 'they are here now, they are here now'. I repeated this at length, wondering what my brother knew and why it had made such an impact on him. I continued with the chant 'they are here now, they are here now' and continued until I fell asleep.

***

Chapter Four

NEOLA MARTON

A few years had passed since the terror of the beating that took place behind the church down at the river. I also found out who the group or gang were. The scariest thing was what they stood for, which seemed to be, lots of hate and to cause as much damage as possible. I also found out that they were called Skinheads or Boneheads as we dubbed them. I think it was only truthful and proper for me to say that in our young and impressionable minds, we were at best confused about these Skinhead gangs.

For example, a few years ago, I told you about a bright new pair of monkey boots, which I pointed out, were a cheap version of the real thing, which were Doc Martins boots. You may also remember that these boots played a vital role in me having one of the most memorable situations of my younger years, oh yes! I remember that day fondly.

I beg of you to please, please have patience with me as I digress once again. I am meant to be making it clear to you the point of confusion regarding the Skinhead gangs and us. Well, if monkey boots were the cheap option to the real Doc Martins, then at some level, we either wanted to be Skinheads or even worse, respected them. I can vividly remember my older brother mumbling under his breath when I asked mum for a pair of those boots, I remember him and his friends saying to mum, 'you need to tell him, you need to tell him!'.

I confess to not being sure where the image of wearing monkey boots came from, but I do know that it was something I felt I needed to have. Suddenly, a thought came to mind. It was a thought about all those cloud formations and, particularly, the similarity between my cloud formation and those of the members of the Skinhead group. At length, I pondered on the idea of why my fluffy white cloud was so unlike my brother's cloud, and that of the two guys I described when in deep discourse on my road a few years back.

The clouds I used to describe as being discoloured, which I had compared to my fluffy white cloud a few years ago, no longer seemed to be discoloured at all. In fact, these silky black clouds seemed to have elegance, charm, and power all of their own. I, for the first time, started to truly wonder why my cloud and my brother's cloud were so different. We both sprung from the same tree, we lived, ate and slept in the same home, so why the difference? The very answer to this question would come to me much, much later in life.

It was the morning after the day before, and it was time for me to leave for school. I never used to eat breakfast, and many of the working-class children that lived in our area never ate breakfast either. I must point out that this was not due to any wholesale neglect on the part of our parents, but more a case of circumstance. Many of the parents in our area obtained manual jobs which were largely factory work and, in particular, working on conveyor belts. This meant that our parents had to leave home at an ungodly hour of the morning and arrive home late.

Well, on this particular morning, whilst walking to school, which incidentally, was on the same path the Skinheads used all those years ago leading to the river where that guy was so brutally beaten, I used to think about that guy almost every day wondering if he was still alive or worse dead. I walked down the path at the back of the church and crossed the bridge leading to my school. On the path in the distance, I could see the shape, roll and bump of Neola Marton. Please allow me the great honour of describing to you this young girl's most amazing gifts that could only be given by Him and/or that which creates all things beautiful.

Neola Marton, Neola Marton, for her racial background, it was not very common to have the accentuated parts of the anatomy in this way, it was much more common for members of my racial background to have what were deemed as being oversized body parts and/or appendages. Well, in this case, it can only be said that He and/or that which creates all things truly beautiful gave Neola's construction his full attention. Her shoulders were strong, she had large, well-formed breasts, and the smallest of waistlines followed by what can only be described as a monster backside! Oh! If only you could see this thing roll, and it would seem at times, she could barely manage all the gifts bestowed upon her.

Well, I had made up my mind that very morning that very little school work was going to be done on that day. I was hell-bent on bunking as many classes as I could and hoped that I would instead be spending that time behind the P.E block with Neola Marton. I walked at a pace to catch up with this most amazing figure, I wanted my large hands and fingers to be feeling and fondling as much of her sexy form as possible. My pace quickened, and finally, I found myself no more than a few steps behind her. Just as I was about to take the final step level with Neola, she turned and to my utter surprise said, 'good morning'. I wondered how she knew I was there. I thought did I not wash well enough and maybe smelt, but no I was confident that the voice of my mother in my head telling me how to take a good wash never left me. I asked, 'how did you know it was me coming up behind you?'. To this, she replied, 'I could feel your eyes on me'. I said, 'from way back there you could feel my eyes on you?' She replied, 'was I correct or not, did you or did you not have your eyes trained on my backside while walking along the path?'. I could do nothing more than tell the truth and confess it all to her.

Man! I thought, can feelings really travel like that? But the truth was evident, she was correct; I only had one thing on my mind that very morning. I inquired as to her disposition on this bright and cheerful morning to ascertain what kind of mood she was in, she said with a warm smile, 'I am feeling rather good this morning actually'. At this point, a couple of the older boys in our school came past and greeted Neola, 'GOOD MORNING' they exclaimed, Neola with a greeting equal to theirs replied 'GOOD MORNING'. I could not help but mumble under my breath, 'push off, this one is for me today'.

I noticed the older boys having the same coloured clouds as my older brother; they were still not the same as mine, even though we shared the same racial background. I looked up at my cloud and that of Neola's and could see that they were the same fluffy white clouds. As we walked, I could see that both our clouds seemed to be bright, fluffy and were merging as we walked further. This was, for me, a good sign as I remembered years back when you were in the presence of certain girls and your clouds merged. That was a sure sign that you were going to have some kind of physical interaction.

As we entered the front gate of the school, we walked a short distance, and then the bell rang for first registration. Well, it seemed like synergy because we both said at once, 'are you going to registration?'. We both laughed at the thought that we were both thinking the same thing, 'Nah!' I said, 'what about you?'. Neola paused for a moment and said, 'if we don't go to registration where will we go to and what will we do?'. Well, my mind kicked into overdrive with the many thoughts of just exactly where and what to do if we indeed did not go to registration. My heart rate bumped up a couple of beats, my Towley had started to do its thing yet again, but the only difference now was that I was fully aware of its capabilities and its intentions.

The second bell sounded, and the last few stragglers, which included me and Neola started to make our way to the building where our form class was found. We all seemed to be dragging our heels, almost like we were all waiting for someone to make the first move and change direction to move away from the form class and indeed, registration. Missing class becomes much harder if you actually went to registration and then slipped out afterwards. Just as there were a few steps left to take, I tugged on Neola's arm and beckoned her towards the P.E block. It was like running the gauntlet as we had to traverse the whole playground to get there.

Neola looked at me with a look of what I can only describe as contentment; we made up our minds that day that it would not be a school registration day, well at least not for us. We turned away from our form block building and walked briskly across the playground, all the while we hoped not to hear the voice of Mr Dee. Now it would take a whole book in itself to tell you about that very nasty, nasty piece of work they called Mr Dee. Suffice to say he was from the Northern parts of England, the parts were no-nonsense men came from, or at least that was until they lived down south for too long.

We briskly made our way across the playground and made it to the P.E block. Neola was just a few steps ahead of me as I purposely walked a little slower than Neola to gain a full view of those so round and luscious bottom cheeks. As she walked, I could not help but think there must be some kind of genetic cross over, because a girl from her particular racial group rarely had physiology of this kind. I guess this only made it seem that much more appealing to the eye, it seemed somewhat out of place but yet so tantalising. We finally made it behind the P.E block without being detected by Mr Dee; things were looking up for me on this particular morning.

We made our way to the blind spot that could not be seen by any other part of the school, but I was later to discover that just because it was a blind spot to the school did not automatically make it a blind spot to the rest of the world. Verily I shall give you the gorier details in full a little later, but for now, it is all about Neola and the fact that we were going to spend the whole morning together, and that at least could take up to lunchtime, getting it on. Now I must confess that this account I am about to tell you, I fear my story will not be as exciting as my earlier account in the adventure playground some years back, but I can and will assure you that the pleasure therefrom was equal to none.

Neola had chosen to take the wall on this occasion, Oh! Man! with a posture that suggested I was in for a major session. Now you will, I hope, remember from my earlier account in the adventure playground all those years ago, that one of our cultural musts is that you have a great command of your pelvic movements. It has been known to go as far as being the sole reason for having and/or chasing a particular girl because many shaky relationships have ended over the inability of one member of the couple not being able to gyrate their pelvic area in the appropriate manner. This was a very important skill to have command of in the late 1970s and onwards. Wow! I was just about to put my pelvic skills into action.

Well, I can also at this very stage inform you that though Neola was not of the same racial background as me, she did not only possess the genetics of a member of my cultural community, but she had the pelvic power too. Now as funny as you may find this, I too pondered on the question of how she knew how to move so well, and then all of a sudden it hit me, Neola had the same experience as me and the girl who lived a few doors down from my house! I thought damn, we have been doing our work. It was like she had been trained especially for the job. She placed her back against the wall and dropped her school bag off her shoulder with a thump as it fell onto the ground. Neola looked at me as though to say, 'come and get it, cowboy'. She parted her legs just enough for me to get one of my legs between. As I made my approach my heart racing ten to the dozen, I purposely slipped my leg between hers, and it was almost like the 5th of November, Guido Fawkes.

Well, as I have previously mentioned, this account will not indeed make good reading as the account had much more to do with feelings of unquantifiable pleasure. Suffice to say, Neola and I pressed our pelvic bones together and commenced a bump and grind marathon. We started fairly slowly and then built up to heavy kissing and petting. I would have one hand on at least one buttock cheek at all times and would move the other hand between her beautifully formed breast and her invitingly hairy Catty at the front.

It was a nice morning and the sun was just making its feelings known, so had the heat that had elevated between us as did the effects of the sun. Neola and I pressed against each other to almost what could only be described as a frenzied state, and this was as good as it gets. We continued to pleasure one another to the point that we had both completely forgotten where we were. With the heat of the sun and the body heat that we both created, we started to loosen and unbutton our shirts, it seemed to happen all in one swift movement but no sooner had a couple of buttons become undone Neola lifted her skirt to reveal the pleasure that lay therein.

I took a small but measured step back to gorge myself on the view that had been afforded to me. Neola had lifted her skirt to the panty level, and I could clearly see the bulge under her panties, which only served to increase my level of excitement. Neola using her forefinger and thumb gracefully slipped her panties to one side to expose her pubescent goodies, I did not need another moment to think as I started to unzip my trousers. I pulled out my already very erect Towley that was full of the lubricant juices that are the precursor for any kind of penetrative sex, or as it is in our case, for rubbing genitalia together in a simulated sex style.

Though I had already experienced full penetrative sex, we had also learnt that non-penetrative sex could be just as good if not better than penetrative sex. Today was a clear bet on the non-penetrative sex option. As I had already mentioned, we both gave very little thought about where and what we were doing. RING! The bell of the first class had just sounded; it was almost like a faint noise in the distance. I took the step forward between Neola's legs, and I could scarcely articulate just how warm and inviting Neola's Catty was, as we set about regaining the heightened pleasure we had before that moment's pause.

I can say with certain boastfulness that it did not take too long before the heightened pleasure returned. The feeling of our genitalia touching and rubbing against each other cannot be easily described, but I do sincerely hope that you, the reader, have had the fortunate occurrence of experiencing the pleasures of what had been dubbed by us at the time as DRY SEX. Dry sex, there was nothing that could beat it. In fact, it made up the base functions of the many parties that would take place in my particular cultural background as it lent itself to music such as slow Soul songs, Lovers Rock and Calypso. Anyone or all of these music forms combined was a sure recipe for heat and passion.

I digress once more and have left the process of telling you about my morning's encounter with Neola Marton. As you have been informed, the bell to the end of the first period had gone, but this did not affect the passion that was being unleashed behind the P.E block. Neola and I continued to escalate the intensity of our sexual exploits. Neola's skirt remained up and access was never made an issue. My pelvic movement had shifted up a gear, and it was clear that I meant business, I gyrated, and rolled, and ground my Towley against Neola's moist Catty to great effect.

I could see Neola's eyes rolling to the back of her head; she was truly in a good place at that moment in time. By now, my excitement and pleasure mixed together gave space, sense and time very little, if any meaning at all. My trousers had reached my knees by this point and my underpants were not too far behind them. We continued to kiss, fondle and gyrate to the maximum of our abilities piling on pleasure after pleasure, tingling feeling after tingle. You may find this next part a little strange accounting for my actions. In the midst of all that pleasure and lust, I took a moment to inspect the status of my cloud. Bump, grind, gyrate and tingle I could still not help myself from checking on its status. Well, suffice to say, there it was fluffy as ever, white to the tune and it stood completely intertwined with Neola's cloud.

My temporary lapse from what was taking place was only for a second or two, but it somehow felt like it was for much longer. After the inspection, I returned to the job at hand, though I had taken my mind off the job for only a second or two, the momentum we had built up had not been affected. We continued as we had started, by now Neola had made mincemeat of my waistline and I felt like I needed the support of the wall for a little while. I summarily changed places with Neola, and we seemed to make the swap keeping the same rhythm as we had been making all morning. By now it is fast approaching the end of the second period that would mean that it was going to be the first playtime for the whole school, but Neola and I had very little, if any, sense of time at this point.

Places swapped, we continued our sexual onslaught on one another, ever-escalating the tension and sexual heat. It almost seemed as if there could be no more pleasure to be found on this very earth that could be compared to those feelings. As I have already said, sense, time and space had no meaning. Suddenly I looked over Neola's shoulder to discover that, although we were not visible to the rest of the school, we were very much visible to the houses that lined the street that led to our school from the opposite way from where we came into school.

I noticed that a kitchen roller blind was at half-mast then suddenly went to full-mast; I could make out that there were two heads in the window watching us. I was overtaken with only a moment of shock to see these faces in the window. I knew that it should have been the point in which I needed to stop this session behind the P.E block, but the sheer pleasure of this moment made it impossible for me to disclose this to Neola.

I thought just a few more pumps and we would have to stop before the bell of the second period was to sound, so in earnest, I sought to have just a few more pumps bearing in mind my trousers were at my ankles, my underpants the same, and Neola had tucked her skirt into her waistband ever so tightly. I noticed a shadow at the corner of the P.E block, and with a fast brain calculation, I could not explain it. An even greater sign you may think for stopping this sexual escapade, but no I let the pleasures of the flesh rule and was about to pay dearly for it. Suddenly from behind the corner where I had seen the shadow, appeared Mr Dee! 'Michael and Neola! What the hell do you think you are doing?'. My eyes opened as wide as two saucers and Neola's was much the same, we both froze on the spot. I noticed that the two faces in the kitchen window had been pointing in our direction as if to direct someone towards us, but alas as I previously mentioned, the pleasure had made utter soup of my senses. At speed, Mr Dee had made his way to us and shouted in his Northern accent 'to the Headmasters office the pair of you!'. Frantically, I bent down to pull up my underpants and trousers while Neola tried to find the bottom of her skirt that she had tucked so well into her waistband.

Mr Dee grabbed both of us by the scruff of the neck and dragged us across the playground to the main building where the Headmaster's office was found. I was still trying to pull my trousers up, and Neola was trying to pull her skirt back down. Suddenly, as we are halfway across the playground, the bell to end the second period sounded, this was a bell that did not need to be sounded twice because everyone in the class would have packed their books away at least five minutes before the bell would sound. It was like a plague from almost every orifice, it seemed like the sight and sound of our peers coming out to play whilst Mr Dee still had us by the scruff of our necks leading us to the Headmaster's office.

Great cheers arose from each and everybody that saw us as we were being led to our fate. By the time we had gotten across the playground and to the entrance of the main building, we had succeeded in finally putting our clothes back on. We both arrived outside the Headmaster's office and were told to sit down. Mr Dee knocked on the Headmaster's door and went inside. Neola and I sat there in total silence. My hands were shaking, and I could see Neola's hands doing the same.

I think it was a case of adrenaline and fear mixed together that made it impossible for speech. We both sat there in utter silence and then the door to the Headmaster's office opened and out came Mr Dee, 'get inside the Headmaster's office the pair of you' he shouted at the top of his voice. Neola and I got up and made our way into the Headmaster's office and closed the door behind us.

**

Chapter Five

THE HEADMASTER'S OFFICE

NEOLA and I sat in the Headmaster's office. We afforded each other only one single glance and it was as if we had not just spent the best part of two hours in a deep embrace. All the while, the Headmaster had not so much as raised his head towards our direction. I can confess that at this point, I had no idea how we were going to manage this situation at hand. I hoped, at the very least, that my co-defendant would at least tow the same line as whoever was asked to speak first.

The Headmaster still had his head down doing his paperwork, but then he slowly started to raise his head and looked straight at us. 'Well, Michael can you tell me what the devil you think you two were up to behind the P.E block?'. I tried my best to get some moisture to wet my lips so that I was able to answer, but on each attempt, I was unable to access my saliva banks and my mouth remained dry.

Mr Batten raised his head erect and in a forceful and purposeful tone exclaimed, 'Michael I have asked you a question'. However, I was still at this point trying to get some kind of moisture to my lips but on each occasion, I failed, 'what's the matter?' Mr Batten asked, 'has the cat got your tongue?' I looked in Neola's direction hoping that maybe she might intervene but alas Neola's head stayed down staring at the floor between her legs; there was no help to be found there.

At last, I finally managed to utter a single word, and in advance I apologise for the senselessness of the word I uttered. For some unexplained reason, the only word I could utter was 'BUT!' 'BUT!' Mr Batten exclaimed, 'What in the universe has the word BUT got to do with you being behind the P.E block skipping classes?' I mustered up all my strength to speak again only to find me saying 'BUT!' once more. I knew I was in for it at this point; Mr Batten enquired 'are you trying to be funny' and claimed I had lost the ability to speak at my age.

I could not start to think why he was not asking Neola what happened since both of us were caught behind the P.E block, but not so, the focus remained solely on me. Finally, my saliva glands had occasioned me with their presence and were able to form a basic sentence. 'Well,' I said, 'we were not doing anything at all'. 'Am I to understand that you both were not at registration and the first two periods of the morning, and you were behind the P.E block doing nothing?'. Mr Batten asked, 'do I look stupid to you?'. A devilish second voice came to mind saying, 'actually you do look a bit stupid in that Batman cape you're wearing'.

Back then, even in comprehensive schools, there was a little pomp and ceremony surrounding the Head's position in the educational structure. Mr Batten continued his one-sided onslaught. 'Michael, I am asking you again, what were you and Neola doing behind the P.E block?'. By now, I had full command of my vocal capacity. I thought about my big brother and all the older boys I had heard talking about when you get caught doing something wrong, they all say the same thing and that was you must stick to your story and not change it. They even went as far as having a saying which said - you must stick to your guns, Blue is Blue, and it could never, in the middle of an interrogation, become Green.

Mr Batten continued with his line of questioning while the whole time Neola kept her head down, which seemed to be working because she was never asked a single question. I thought that maybe I should adopt this same strategy, and then maybe the questioning will stop. As I lowered my head, the sound of thunder rang out, and it seemed to engulf the entire main building. This was the sound of Mr Batten shouting at the very top of his voice. 'For the last time, I am going to ask you what were you two doing behind the P.E block?'. I was so startled by the sheer veracity of his voice that my head immediately regained its original upright state.

I could do very little to respond, I was completely frozen at this point and used my peripheral vision to see that Neola still had her head firmly down. It was as if she had suddenly become mute or some other ill fate had fallen upon her again. From my peripheral vision, I could also see my cloud, strange as it seemed as the interrogation continued, I could see my and Neola's cloud steadily parting, it was happening as I spoke. Every time I said something, our clouds would separate a little more, I thought to myself 'what could this be?'. It was as if, through our clouds, I was being excommunicated, something I confess to have never witnessed before.

Mr Batten then made a statement that made my eyes open as wide as saucers; he said, 'I have been advised that you were taking advantage of this girl behind the P.E block'. 'Taking advantage,' I said, 'yes taking advantage' Mr Batten said. 'No' I said, keeping to what I had been taught by the older boys that you must never change your story at any point in an interrogation. 'Me and Neola were not doing anything behind the P.E block'. Mr Batten responded by saying 'do you mean to say that Mr Dee is a liar?'. 'No, No I am not calling him a liar, but we were not doing anything, and I certainly was not taking advantage of Neola'. I thought why at this point would she not step in and say that I was not taking advantage of her, but nothing would come from her at all.

Mr Batten continued to assert the fact that I had been taking advantage of Neola behind the P.E block. The whole time our clouds were continuing to part and for the first time, I started to see a distinct change in the colour of my cloud. For the first time, my fluffy white cloud had started to become tainted and tinges of grey also started to appear. 'Do you know that this is a very serious accusation if it is indeed found that you have been taking advantage of Neola Marton you will be in grave trouble?'. I thought in my head that this could not be happening, Neola knew very well that I was not taking advantage of her, in fact, it could be said that it was as much her as it was me.

Mr. Batten continued to say that he did not only have the word of Mr Dee to support his case, but he also had a statement from a member of the public to corroborate. The witness had telephoned into the school, and it was Mr Dee who intercepted the call, he was then directed to the exact place in which you were found. It turned out that it was the two people seen in the kitchen window that had made the dreaded call; I knew I should have stopped at that point. But the thrill, excitement and the feel of Neola made it near impossible.

I could barely take it anymore; I stood up from my chair and said to Neola 'are you not going to say anything?'. All the while Neola continued to keep her head down and said nothing. This could not be happening I thought to myself she has got to step in and help me out, the tone had escalated in the Headmaster's office, and words of rape suddenly entered the room. Mr Batten shouted and told me to sit back down, 'you are in no position to make any demands here, can you not see that Neola is frightened, shocked and scared'. Mr Batten then asked if Neola was alright and if she needed anything to drink or whether she needed to see the nurse.

As the Headmaster was speaking to Neola, I noticed that both his cloud and Neola's cloud had started to merge. I was astounded as to what this could be? I had never seen the merging of an adult and a child's cloud before or any cloud for that matter. I wondered what this could mean, I had momentarily forgotten about the grave charge that had just been levelled against me. I simply could not find a single reason why Mr Batten and Neola's cloud were merging and all the while, my cloud and Neola's cloud were separating. My cloud, as I previously mentioned, had also been changing from its fluffy white cloud to an off white, almost turning to a grey colour.

Mr Batten continued at length to assert the idea that I was taking advantage of Neola. He talked about possibly having to inform both our parents and that they may even have to involve the Police. I thought to myself, how a morning of such unquestionable pleasure could suddenly turn so dire. There seemed to be some sort of pattern here. I noticed from my early years' experience that after each and every pleasurable moment came equal amounts of sadness or pain. The time after Katy in the adventure playground came with the sadness of the brutal beating. This time it was the accusation of rape against Neola who had not been in danger of any sort.

By now Neola had started to cry, and Mr Batten took out a tissue from the tissue box and offered it to her. For the very first time in the whole proceedings, Neola lifted her head, all the while crying as if some terrible fate had befallen her. 'Thank you' she said as she stretched out her arm to receive the tissue. I felt a mixture of emotions building up inside me, rage on the one hand, dismay on the other, here I was being accused of taking advantage of someone and it could not have been any further from the truth. Mr Batten seemed to be very concerned with Neola, and for a moment I noticed him giving her a little wink, all the while their clouds were merging even more with one another.

I think it is important to point out that both Neola and the Headmaster shared the same racial background as each other, not that this on its own should mean anything, but I thought it important based on the fact that I did not share the same racial background as Mr Batten or Neola. Neola took the tissue and blew her nose; she then reassumed the same posture as before, which was head down and say nothing. Mr Batten politely asked if Neola wanted to go to the nurse to which she replied in a sheepish and tearful voice 'yes, yes I would like to go to the nurse please'.

All the while, Neola was crying as though this very dangerous and nasty accusation was somehow true. It all happened in but a moment, Neola had left the Headmaster's office and it was just me left holding the baby, as we used to say in those days. I could see the cloud formations of both Mr Batten and Neola's slowly pulling apart as she left the office, I could not help but say, under my breath, that he was taking her side. The door shuts behind Neola, and Mr Batten turned to me and resumed his interrogation, 'so Michael' he said, 'I have an independent witness statement plus that of a teacher that you were taking advantage of that innocent girl'.

'Do you realise the gravity of your actions?' Mr Batten asked. I had by now gained full control of my ability to speak, I said rather boldly, as I felt that there was not much to lose at this point, it seemed that the school, so-called witness and Mr Dee had made up their mind that I was guilty, without going through the legal process and without a shred of evidence. I used to hear the older boys and my big brother often talk about cases such as these. It seemed that if you shared the same racial background as myself and sported a black silky cloud, you were more than ten times likely to be stopped by the police, and in some cases taken away in what was called a Black Moriya. I continued to plead my innocence and kept on saying that we were not doing anything behind the P.E block.

Mr Batten sat back down and started to look at a piece of paper on his deck, so then I took a moment to re-examine the status of my cloud and noticed that it had maintained this new greyish tone. I could go as far as saying that it was in the process of changing colour, suddenly there was a knock at the door and in came the secretary who said to Mr Batten, 'they're here now' and with that, she turned and left the room. I did not take much notice of this statement as I assumed it would be a parent of one of the children complaining about the quality of the school lunches, I was just about to learn that was not the case at all.

Mr Batten put the piece of paper back on his desk and informed me that I would be suspended immediately and that I was not to return to school for a whole week. Suspended! I thought. Just a short time ago, I was between the thighs and warm bosom of Neola Marton, and now it looked like my whole world was about to end. It seemed like I had lost the ability to speak again and was unable to respond to what I had just heard. Mr Batten informed me that 'the secretary is in the process of writing a letter for you to take to your parents'. For the first time today, I thought about my mum and what she might do to me for getting suspended from school.

I thought to myself that it could surely not get any worse than it is now when suddenly there was another knock at the door which I presumed was the secretary with the letter to mum, but how wrong I was. The door opened and in walked two Officers of the Law or the BEAST! as we dubbed them at that particular time in recent history. Two officers in full uniform entered the room. As the officers entered, they both removed their hats, my heart sunk, what on earth could these officers be doing here.

It was to become evident to me in a very short space of time; the reason the two officers of the law were in Mr Batten's office. As the two officers took a position beside the Headmaster, Mr Batten said 'I tried to ask you what happened behind the P.E block and you kept saying nothing. Well, I can't help you now'. 'You can't help me' I thought to myself, that's rich coming from you. You just helped Neola then why not me. The BEAST! started with their so-called charge of rape, just the very mention of such a word when it concerned me and Neola sounded more like a crime than anything else.

For a moment, a calm came over me as I said to myself that Neola would tell them the truth as it was because surely she was not going to let me get into trouble for something as serious as a rape charge. I was to find out a little later how wrong I was, and it seemed from that point on that everything that was said in that office was one big blur. All I could think of was how I could hide this suspension from my mum. It seemed to go on forever, but I remember the last words being, 'we need to interview you again, but it will be at the police station'.

I remember suddenly coming too and being handed a letter from Mr Batten about the suspension and the reason for the suspension. I had been in the Headmaster's office for such a long time that the rest of the school day was just about to end; the bell for the last period had just sounded which meant that another school day had ended. I took the letter from Mr Batten and started the long walk back from the main block to the playground, which led to the main gates. I have to confess that I did not see Neola leave school that day, and even though it looked like she had completely deserted me, I could still not help but think about her curves and the feelings to be had there from.

I walked along the same path that only a few hours ago held the magic and splendour of a great day, which turned out to be a day of total dread. I wished that one of those older boys who greeted Neola that morning had been lucky to hold her attention, or not so lucky in my case. I got to the bridge that forever holds the memory of that fateful day of the river beating, and crossed it, just before I got to the back of the church. I remembered a large Horse Chestnut tree being the last thing you would see before you got to my road.

I took the letter out of my pocket and placed it in a crevice in the tree; I made sure that I was not seen doing it or at least that was what I thought. I made my way home and waited until either of my sisters or my brother got back from school. While I waited for them, I was left with an abundance of time to inspect my cloud.

MICHAEL J. CHARLES

By now, my cloud was half white and half grey, the fluffy side was as I always remembered it to be, but the new grey side was all a mystery to me. I went upstairs to my room and did as I always did, which was lie on my back and look up at the ceiling, and just as in every case, I fell asleep.

***

77

Chapter Six

THE JOY OF SEX

D AY two of the suspension and I was sure I could get away with not telling my mum about the horrid ordeal. Three more working days to go and no one would be the wiser. Well on the morning of the third day, the sounds in the house seemed to be pretty normal, the sound of the radio playing as my mother and father both got ready to go to work, then out of the blue the sound of my mother's voice calling onto me to wake up.

This then was a little strange as we had at least an hour and a half of sleep time before we had to get up to have our daily wash. 'Michael' my mother called 'wake up and come downstairs at once'. My heart immediately sunk, my brother rolled over and looked at me and said, 'you must be in for it because mum does not usually wake us up at this time of the morning'. 'Michael', she shouted, 'please don't let me have to call you again'. To this, I immediately jumped out of bed and ran straight downstairs, both my parents were in the kitchen, and they did not look at all happy, in fact, the look on their faces told a story.

I greeted my parents with a bright and beaming good morning, to which I received little more than a grunt. My father had to leave earlier than my mother, so at this point, my father kissed my mother on the cheek and bade her goodbye. My father did not afford me the same salutation and summarily left for work; I by now had sensed an ensuing problem but could not be sure exactly what it was. 'Michael!' my mother exclaimed, 'how is school at the moment?' Well, my instincts told me that this enquiry was not at all normal, especially at this ungodly hour of the morning.

I suddenly remembered the advice of my older brother and the older guys that he used to spend most of his time with. Never disclose anything before you are asked and remember to stick to it once you have given something up. Blue is Blue, is all I could say to myself when mum repeated the question. 'Michael, I have asked you how is school at the moment?'. 'Well!' I replied, and no sooner had I said that mother exclaimed 'well! is not an answer'. 'Ok,' my mother said, 'I will make it a little easier for you. How has school been this week?'. My heart rate raced thinking with only three days of the suspension to go; she couldn't possibly know I had been suspended from school this week. As I was certain that I had so cleverly disposed of the evidence that pertained to it.

I attempted a reply and said 'well, it's the same as usual'. 'Oh!' my mother replied 'so when I come to the school this afternoon to watch the musical recital, I can expect to see you in the hall with the other parents and children?'. I knew at that very moment that I was in the gravest of positions. I pondered on the very idea of telling my mother the truth about my suspension but could only hear the voice of my brother saying stick to your guns. The guns that say Blue is Blue once you have said it, all the while my mother is still waiting for a reply. I looked above me and lo and behold my cloud was above my head, but since the time with Neola Marton and the Headmaster, my cloud has been changing colour.

My cloud had begun to take on a more greyish tone and was no longer that fluffy white ball of candy floss that I had become used to.

I distinctly remember looking at my mother's cloud and thinking how amazingly black it looked, I wondered at length whether my cloud was beginning to turn the same way as the older boys who shared the same racial background as me? My thoughts returned to the experience in the Headmaster's office with Neola Marton, and the fact that Neola and the Headmaster's clouds had temporally merged. As my conscious thoughts started to come back to me, I realised that I had to apply some fast action thinking, and I would need to work out why I was not to be seen at the recital that was due to happen at school on this very day.

The time was moving ever so fast, so it seemed on this very morning, and I could see that it was only a matter of time before my mother would leave for work. I could not think of a single thing that could save me from the impending interrogation that would follow about me not being present at the recital that afternoon. My mother seemed to accept that I had not responded to her question that was if she would see me at the recital later that day.

With this, I heard my mother say goodbye to all of us who were either in a half state of sleep or busy getting ready to start their day. I bade my mother goodbye and wished her a very good day, to which she replied, 'I hope that can be applied to you too?'. And with that, my mother left the house. I immediately went upstairs and returned to the bed I shared with my older brother, he by this time was lucky enough to have gotten a space in the bathroom and was busy getting ready to start his day.

I did as I had done so many times before, which was to lie on my back on my bed looking up at the ceiling and inspecting my cloud. I started to think back to when the guy had been beaten up by the gang of boys by the river behind our house. I was thinking about him in relation to my cloud and its changing form, I suddenly realised that the guy who was being beaten up did not have a cloud formation that resembled the one from the group that was set about him, nor did he share one that was likened to me or mine.

It became clear to me at this point that the guy who was being beaten up, only had an outline of a cloud, but it seemed to have no filling therein, I pondered on this idea for some time and could not think why this would be the case. It seemed to me that everybody had a cloud and it also seemed to me that all clouds had a filling of some sort, but that was not the case here, I pondered until I drifted off to sleep.

I suddenly gasped for air as though I had been held underwater, or some similar misfortune had occasioned me. By now, the whole house was empty, as my brother and two sisters had left for school already. I regained my senses and made my way to the bathroom, all the while, I contemplated the idea of how I was to be present at the musical recital whilst being suspended from school. As I washed, the thought suddenly dawned on me that, all I had to do was find a way to sneak into school just before the recital and not stay long enough afterwards in order not to be detected by the Headmaster and Mr Dee. I had decided, this was the plan, and all I had to do was execute it, and all would turn out fine. I made my way out of the bathroom and back into my bedroom humming a nondescript tune in my head, feeling pleased that I had indeed hatched a plan that I felt could do no less than succeed.

As I continued to get ready, I started moisturising my skin when suddenly and involuntarily the thought of Neola Marton came to mind, even though she was the reason I had been suspended. I could not help but get lost in her more than perfect form, her shape so uncharacteristic for her racial background, but it never failed to get a second glance from anyone she happened to pass. I did indeed ask you to have patience with me, in my story about a cloud; this then I impress upon you once again to have patience with me.

As I am indeed certain, you have by now learnt the full meaning of the word Towley. Well, I fear this will then be one of those moments of a recount, as I continued to ponder on the ever so perfect shape of Neola Marton's body. I almost went faint at the very loss of blood that seemed to be draining from the top half of my body, as I looked down, it became apparent where all this blood was rushing to. Needless to say, I was very proud of what my eyes had befallen upon, pulsating and throbbing quite intently, there was scarcely room for not even one single drop more of blood therein, it was as if my, oh so dear to me, Towley would explode under the pressure.

You may at this point think my account to be rather funny, but I in no uncertain terms, seek to make it clear to you that this situation I find myself in, is anything but funny. I tried to think of something else, anything Tennis, Rugby, Golf, one of these should do it I thought, alas it was not the case and what little blood I had left in my body had now made its way down to my Towley. I knew from past experiences that this was not going to subside on its own accord. Well, I knew I didn't have to sneak into school for the next few hours. So, this in my mind allowed me ample time in which to deal with this rigid predicament I found myself in, so I gazed at myself in the mirror behind the door of the bedroom I shared with my brother.

I must, if you will allow me this moment of self-indulgence, say that my form was pretty good and a force to be reckoned with in my opinion. At length I continued to moisturise myself all the while looking on proudly at my inflexible Towley, I pondered on the fact that I had been clearly betrayed by Neola Marton, but yet her uncompromising form could still attain a reaction such as this. My attention had returned to the issue at hand, my Towley, which I was certain, was going to simply explode if I did not do something with it as soon as possible. It then came to me in a flash! Both my sisters had left the house which meant I had access to the library of books to be found in their bedroom, between the selection of Mills & Boons books would be The Joy of Sex which was a weekly encyclopaedia of our body plus the labelling of those parts.

This I would accompany with a copy of the Kays Catalogue, which I am sure you're aware has the knicker and bra section. There would always be a pair of see-through panties and bras to be found in this section, this coupled with The Joy of Sex books would make for useful visual stimuli. Now satisfied that my body was fully moisturised, I set off to my sisters' room, I pushed the door open to find an almighty mess, there were clothes everywhere socks, bras, shirts, panties, you name it, it was there. I mumbled to myself through all the mess left behind, that if my brother and I left our bedroom like that, we would not hear the end of it that I knew for sure.

Well, I fingered my way through the Mills & Boons section of the bookshelves, and my fingers came across the first copy of The Joy of Sex. I fingered my way some more and found a second copy, all I needed now I thought to myself was the Kays catalogue and I would be set. So just at the end of the second shelf, I could see the corner of that trusted thick but oh so useful catalogue, I took all three books down and lay them on the floor. It was a copy of The Joy of Sex on the left side, the catalogue in the centre and the second copy of The Joy of Sex on the right side.

It seemed I was all set since there had been no change at all to the pulsating and throbbing intensity of my Towley, I took one final look around the room as if to check if there could be someone else in the room. Well, with the vision of Neola Marton firmly etched in my mind, I stood above my strategically placed visual aids lovingly placed on the floor and set about my work. At first, I started very slowly with long and purposeful strokes being sure to experience the full length and ensuring the greatest amount of pleasure.

I knew from previous experience that as I turned the pages of all three books respectively, the visual stimuli would increase and would surely lead me to my end goal, which was to return my blood supply to its original state of keeping my whole body functioning. So, at length, I continued to pull and stroke on my stiffness, and it would seem that even more blood was leaving the core of my body and rushing towards rigidness. By now I had completely lost all track of time and largely forgotten just how much trouble I was in concerning my suspension. I had this feeling that this was destined to be no short affair, summarily I continued with the work at hand.

I bent over still pulling and stroking as I reached down to turn the first pages, The Joy of Sex book on the left side revealed two images. On the left side of the page was an anatomical image of a female body, and on the right side of the page was the image of a naked female body. The catalogue had lots of pictures of women in what was called French Knickers, and these would always remind me of the athletic sports shorts that would be worn by the girls who made the county athletics team. Finally, on the right side was the second copy of The Joy of Sex, which displayed a naked man on the left page, which I have to say, I didn't much care for at this particular point in time.

On the page on the right side was a picture of a naked woman which sported the bushiest Catty I had ever seen; this then had the effect of reminding me of one of my primary school teachers by the name of Miss Francisco. I can vividly remember Hooly, Fod and myself being in the swimming pool looking up at Miss Francisco's bush and gasping at how far down her inside leg it grew. Verily I plead with you to have patience with my long-winded account of my story about a cloud, but in truth, it is the only way to explain it to you fully, that you may indeed truly understand.

I pulled and tugged and stroked my rigid Towley, I was sure it could simply not get any bigger but how wrong I was. As I turned more pages, the more my Towley would take on blood, and again I was sure it would never reach the crescendo the urethra was just too tight. I had simply come too far now to turn back. I turned the pages on all three books in rapid succession, and lo! I was met with the ideal images on all three accounts.

The first publication sported the image of a naked lady laying on her back with her legs spread wide apart, the second one featured the front and back view of a lady wearing a bikini with thongs, and lastly, the third publication displayed a lady kneeling on all fours with a very inviting view of her backside and all that was to be found between. Alas then this was just about all I could withstand, and at that very moment, I gave way to all that which had been boiling up inside of me. With a mighty gush, I dispatched my full load which shot fully across the room hitting the bedspread and all across the three publications.

As you may expect, I was held in a paralysed state and was shuddering and trembling with the electrical pulses often associated with self-fulfilment. As with all moments of self-fulfilment comes that lonely moment of realisation of what has just happened. For many, it's the feelings of guilt associated with religion and/or cultural conditioning and for others, it's a feeling of shame or deviance. In my case I fear it was a little bit from each one of the aforementioned maladies, the last thought that rested with me was just how ill-prepared I was to have undertaken this self-indulging plan of action.

As my sense returned to me, it dawned on me that I had not taken in a single tissue or any means with which to clean up the aftermath of my actions. I then had to move very swiftly as my life-giving fluids were rapidly soaking into both the bedspread and the three publications, sprawled across my sisters' bedroom floor. There was very little time to react, I looked around the room only to see all the clothes that were drying on the clothes horse, I thought about trying to make it to the bathroom to get some tissues, but I knew this would mean absolute disaster for me, the bedspread and the publications.

Alas, I reached out to the first thing at hand, which then happened to be a pair of my sister's panties. I reached forward and started to dab at the trail that had soiled the bedspread and had one eye on the load that had surely seeped through the pages on the underside of the publications. At this time, I gave very little thought to whom the items belonged to that I had just used to disguise my indiscretion, I summarily started to dab at what was strewn over all three publications, and then started on myself I folded the panty to get the last dry patch on it and set about liberating myself from the mess I had brought forth.

I suddenly thought of the notion of time, I took a glimpse through the mirror at the clock on the wall, and it had occurred to me that if I was to pull off this idea of sneaking back into school for the recital that day, I would need to start heading to school immediately. I gave very little thought as to how I was going to explain what happened to my sister's panties, and why it had been returned to the washing basket a day after the girls washing had been done. I had now cleaned up all that required my attention and then made straight for the bathroom for the second time that morning.

**

Chapter Seven

THE SCHOOL RECITAL

NEEDLESS to say, I revisited the bathroom and made good my escape. As I passed the church that leads to the path, which was on the way to my school and the adventure playground, the thought came to me that it would have to be an event of mammoth proportions that would indeed get me into school undetected. Suffice to say the latter was indeed the case. I had made it into school, and it seemed to have been with little or no fuss at all, I blended into the fabric of the general school population and not even the teachers looked in my direction, so it seems that I would be able to pull off this cunning plan after all.

I did not mention that I arrived in school just before lunch; the bell gave a shrill sound to signal the start of the lunch hour. The pupils started leaving their form classes and were making their way to the playground and lunch hall, as I stood in the playground just outside the lunch hall, I noticed that some of the pupils that passed me on their way to lunch had the same cloud formation as the boy I had seen all those years ago being set upon by the group of boys that had short hair and steel toe-capped boots. This, to remind you, were the clouds that only seemed to have an outline of a cloud but no filling, they were neither fluffy white nor off white, or grey or indeed the pristine black clouds that I had become so accustomed to seeing.

This then had me pondering for some time, as two questions came to mind. One, why had I not noticed these phenomena before now and, two, what could it possibly be that it only applied to people who shared this same racial background as the boy I had seen being set upon by the short-haired boot wearing group all those years ago? As more and more pupils filed out of their form buildings, the more I would notice the very same phenomena occurring, verily how could I have been so clearly blind before this point? The clouds that had no fillings could be seen by me all around the playground and indeed leading on to the lunch hall too.

I took a glance at my cloud and it was very much there. Still, with each and every moment of each day, it seemed that my cloud had been steadily changing from fluffy white to off white, to grey moving steadily towards the pristine black that I had witnessed with the two boys who shared the same racial background as me on my street some years ago, which was also the same as my older brother and one of my sisters and all of his and her friends. Since the ordeal with Neola Marton and the Headmaster, I noticed a rapid change in the composition of my cloud, but I could not fully understand its apparent manifestation.

As the bulk of pupils had either taken to the playground or the lunch hall, I knew I had only to employ a short period of stealth to make it to the musical recital and avert the possibility of my suspension being discovered by my mother; but far worst still was the prospect of the tongue lashing followed by me having to go upstairs and fetch the very belt that would be used to punish me. 'Gasp' I hear some of you readers say, a tongue lashing is as far as it should go, but this was not the case for people who shared the same racial background as me. I can say with certainty that many of us have and still will have to go and fetch the weapon of our punishment and/or correction.

By now most of the pupils, if not all, had either taken their place in the playground or the lunch hall. I stood in the same spot just outside the lunch hall and watched and listened to the sound of my fellow pupils enjoying their well-earned break from the classroom. I dared not move much because it was not yet certain that I would make it to the musical recital without being detected, after all, I was still very much on suspension.

The constant sound of laughter and shrikes of joy seemed to hypnotise me, and I was transfixed to the spot for a good while it would have seemed. Utter bliss, in fact, the sun was shining brightly in the hypnotic blue sky, then suddenly a sharp stinging sensation had occasioned me on the left side of my face. Flash, just like that, the lights came on, I suddenly gained focus again only to realise that I had been hit fully on the side of the face with a football. Now please allow me this much needed moment to explain what happened next; under ordinary circumstances, a ball being kicked in my face would have caused a situation of very grave retribution, but alas, this could not be the case on this very day.

As I looked down at this ball, the very object of my immediate and unwanted discomfort, it felt as if the whole playground had fallen silent. With my head still looking downwards, I slowly but purposefully started to lift my head and coming towards me I could see one of the pupils who had been playing football. I so wanted to launch into attack mode, but all I could do was to pretend to smile, with gritted teeth, and return his ball. As he made his way back to the other pupils, the sound of the playground suddenly came back sharply to life.

No sooner had life returned to the playground; there was also the sound of the bell signal for the end of the lunch period. I thought to myself only one more period to go, and I will have made it to the musical recital. The only thing that was left for me to do was to find out where I was going to hide and promptly make my way there. I thought behind the P.E. block where Neola Marton and I were caught could be a good place, but I thought against it as I remembered the lady from across the way was the very reason I was in this predicament in the first place, so that was not the place to hide.

I suddenly thought maybe I should use the toilets after the teachers checked them, I could surely make it in there for at least one session. So, I attempted to blend in with the rest of the pupils as they made their way back to the classrooms, as more and more pupils filed out of the lunch hall and into the playground, I noticed that Mr Dee was on his way to inspect the toilets. I thought anytime now, I could still sneak in just behind him and make good my plot to be undetected, luck it would seem was on my side as I saw Mr Dee leaving the toilets and make his way to the other building.

I was able to slip into the building that led to the lunch hall as this was the building that housed the toilets. I had made it into the toilets, and the buzzing of the pupils began to die away. On entering the toilets, I made sure I chose the furthest cubical, as this cubical could not be investigated from below or from above as the other cubicles could. I entered the cubical and put the toilet seat down, so I could use it for sitting. By now the corridors had become silent, and it was just now a case of making it through this one period. I had by now settled in my cubical and was thinking of what I was going to think about for the next 45 minutes when my mind suddenly turned back to the three books I had been using before I came into school. Well needless to say there was very little that could stop me from recounting the immense pleasure of seeing that fully bushed Catty in The Joy of Sex book. Almost at once, my Towley had taken up its rightful state of erected prominence. I thought should I be going through this again? But the thoughts and the stiffness of my Towley appeared to have made a choice for me. I set about the job in hand (again I beg of thee to forgive me this little intended pun), so I took to stroking my Towley at a slow but even pace, I knew that I had at least another 30 minutes to go, so I did not want to arrive too early or even arrive at all. Since I did not have a towel to clean myself after the act, I took to keeping an even rhythm trying to make sure I would not burst with excitement.

On each and every occasion I was about to explode, I would stop all movement altogether. It's funny even though I was upset by the fact that Neola Marton did not stick up for me in the Headmaster's office, I could scarcely help myself from visualising her most exquisite form. My thoughts ran between The Joy of Sex and the utterly perfect form of Neola Marton's body. I continued purposefully, but I must confess that at this moment, I had little idea of the time, but what was clear to me was, the rate in which my dexterity had increased.

As I increased my intensity, a funny thing came to me, for some strange reason, I felt compelled to look up at my cloud. Now in truth, any sane minded person would, I am sure, agree that at moments like these, it is always a good idea to keep your mind on the job. Well, as I said, I looked up at my cloud and there it was, ever-present, never a moment without it. I seemed to remember that I somehow managed to maintain the momentum in hand; this then was a literal statement. As I continued to inspect my cloud it was apparent that a marked change in its appearance had truly taken hold, the off grey had suddenly become battleship grey moving ever on it would seem to a silken pristine black.

By now I saw much less of The Joy of Sex in my mind and instead my mind could only see the irrefutable perfect form of Neola Marton, which led me back to the thought of three days ago in the Headmaster's office. I thought it was in that very room on that very day that my cloud started to change. It was indeed subtle, but nonetheless the very moment of change. I continued to maintain my stiffness, how did I manage to do this I could not say for sure, but it was clear to me that I either needed to stop at this point or let nature take its unrelenting course. Well, as I would imagine, you have guessed, the latter prevailed.

Once again, my focus returned sharply to the job in hand, so as I was in the last cubical in the toilets I at least had full access to the type of toilet paper that could be found in any comprehensive school of that time. The biggest problem with that was that the toilet paper we had to use was much more like tracing paper than the toilet paper you would use at home. Needless to say, I was one of many pupils that went home after school, with a sharp pain in the stomach due to holding off from doing a number two in the toilets at school.

The absolute fear of the prospect of having to clean yourself with that tracing paper, resulted in many of us having to take matters into our own hands, as many days were spent after the lunch period with clenched buttocks holding on for dear life. Well, as for me on this very occasion, I had very little choice, in what I could use to intercept this imminent bodily outpour.

Since I was committed to my chosen path, I set about increasing my stroke ever more purposefully, and the pace and rhythm took hold. I was completely in the throws as Neola Marton had retaken centre stage. I could scarcely make another stroke when what I can only describe as an almighty slap in the back of the neck. This I say not in jest, this was the very sensation of that moment and with tidal force all that which was within, suddenly became apparent.

I confess to the fact that my eyes had rolled up into my head as my knees gave way, and as I stretched out my hands to stabilise myself, I could hear no less than the bell to end the period. Damn! I thought, how could this be? How very inconsiderate to choose this very moment to ring the bell and scupper my second moment of the day. I had to act fast as I could not be late getting out of the toilet, and into the main hall to where the musical recital was going to take place. I say this with absolute certainty; I have never before been caught in such a precarious position, in school as I have now.

A decision had to be made, do I attempt a clean-up job with the tracing paper, or do I do the unthinkable which was to simply fetch old Towley and whip him straight back into my trousers?

I was certain that a clean-up job with the tracing paper would take too long. It was imperative that I came out of the toilet at the same time as the other pupils were in the corridors, so I could make good my plan for being at the musical recital. Once again, I opted for the latter, and in one swift move, I whipped Towley and all its glorious viscose aftermath back into my trousers.

This was by no means a comfortable choice but alas one I had to make if my cunning plan was to succeed. I proceeded to open the cubical door and make my way to a wash basin. I could hear the voices of the other pupils in the corridor, and I knew I had just enough time to wash my hands, which were equally soiled as my recently banished Towley. I set about washing my hands in earnest whilst taking a moment to look in the mirror to check my overall state, I approved of what I saw and completed washing my hands with surgeon-like dexterity as I reached over to the paper towel dispenser, I could not help but ponder that the paper towels would be far more useful inside the actual toilet cubicles.

Well, it was far too late for the use of hindsight now and with one last look in the mirror, I moved to the main toilet door and opened it. It was perfect, it was awash with excited pupils filling the corridor for as far as the eye could see. Some of the pupils were practising the songs they were about to sing, for a moment I had no thoughts about my suspension, what was in my mind was the fact that my mother would be coming to school to see the musical recital and the fact that Neola Marton did not stand up for me in the Headmaster's office three days ago. Gingerly, I made my way to the centre of the pupils nearest to me, making sure I was in the centre as the teachers often lined the edges of the corridors in a bid to keep order. I knew if I could just blend in, I was certain my cunning plan would work, at length, I mingled in with all the other pupils into, at last, the main hall.

We filed in one row after the other all making sure our lines were straight and true, as soon as one line sat down and crossed their legs, another line filed in behind directly behind them. I could see the finish line, and if only I could get to my sitting position, I would have made good this first stage of my cunning plan.

Finally, it was the turn of the line which I was in and the leader of the line set off, as I entered the hall, I discreetly scanned the hall to see if indeed my mother was there. I could not see her, but I did not want to be detected by any of the teachers that may have been aware that I should not be in school at all. We finally got to the row in which we had to sit, we filed in and took our places on the floor. As soon as I took my seat, I again scanned the hall and could see all the other parents, but I could still not see my mother.

I thought perhaps my mother was running late, and at this very moment, a thought crossed my mind, that it could be entirely feasible that my mother was going to make a grand entrance by being late. To add to that very prospect, I would still have to devise a story, to cover the fact that I was not on stage. I realised that I had not thought about the huge problem, of not being on the stage. The Headmaster entered the hall and we all stood up, only to be given a nod, and we immediately sat back down.

The Headmaster started his preamble and I could not help but have one eye on the door, I wondered if my mother was ever going to get here in time for the start of the musical recital. The Headmaster finished his speech and announced that the recital was about to begin. The lights were dimmed, and the pupils for the first piece entered the stage. The first piece was underway, an adagio performed by what could only be described as an apparition of spirit and soul; she was, I think, a sixth former but her name to me was an utter mystery.

She took centre stage and the rest of the group spread across the stage behind her, the lead began to sing, and silence overtook the hall as her lush vocal tones rang out for all to behold. The contributions from others on stage were equally noteworthy and helped to only make for a complete and total sound. The end of the first piece was met with rapturous applause. While delivering her piece, I could not help but notice her cloud, it was huge silken, pristine and jet black this on its own was not very unusual at all were it not for the fact that she did not share the same racial background as me, or the two boys on my road that I described in earlier chapters. In fact, she shared the same racial background as Neola Marton, Katy from the adventure playground and Jenny, who lives a few doors down from my house. I vaguely remember seeing a super cloud of this nature on a boy who shared the same racial background as all four of them, he used to wear a woolly hat that had three stripes on it. I think the colours were red, green and I think the other colour was yellow?

I was sure those colours were the same as the ones my older brother's friends would wear, they used to listen to music with heavy bass lines and when they got up to dance, the hats would bob up and down in time with the music. I assumed the boy maybe listened to the same music as my big brother but wondered at length what the reason could be for the girl on stage to be sporting such a huge silken, pristine black cloud. The ensemble had taken centre stage, and by now I had concluded that my mother was indeed not going to show up after all, I confessed to being very relieved at that very thought as that meant I would no longer have to think of an excuse to explain why I was not on stage.

The ensemble embarked on a medley of allegro, first allegro followed by petit allegro moving into the final grand allegro. The hall had reached a fever pitch, with the pupils all bobbing their heads to the rhythm of the piece. I remember stretching out my leg as it could sometimes get uncomfortable sitting on the floor cross-legged. As I stretched my leg, I noticed a cold sticky sensation on my groin and my thigh, at once I remembered it was the choice I was forced to make in the toilet about forty minutes ago. Just five more minutes of the musical recital remained, and if I could just make it past the teachers, I could run straight home and have a wash before my mother got home.

Well the final piece ended, and the Headmaster retook to the stage, he beamed from ear to ear lapping up all the enthusiasm of all the parents and pupils in the hall. He announced the end of the musical recital and bade the parents a pleasant journey home. I had become a lot more relaxed as it seemed that my cunning plan may have succeeded after all. We all stayed seated and had to wait for the parents to leave first, and then the teachers would direct each line out of the hall. It was the turn of the line I sat in, then the teacher directed us out, and it felt as if I was invisible because not a teacher nor anybody from my actual form class so much as gave me a second glance.

Out into the playground and across to the gate, this seemed all too easy, but it was still not over yet. By now, my confidence had risen as we filed out jubilantly in the corridor; everybody was talking about that solo by the apparition of spirit and soul from the sixth form. She was indeed something to behold. By now, most of us were making our way out of the school gate, and I thought to myself what a masterful and cunning plan, it would seem that the universe had indeed conspired to assist me in the execution thereof. So I arrived at the church just beside my house and could see the proverbial finish line.

I must confess that at this point, I walked with a skip and a bounce, yes, I thought to myself, home and dry, and I did not have to face my mother about the musical recital. I was sure the reason my mother could not attend was due to her boss changing his mind about giving her time off, I walked down my path with an even more animated bounce and skip 'AAH TU LULA AMEN' I said as I pushed the key in the door. I thought I would rush straight upstairs into the bathroom and clean off the aftermath from my handy experience in the cubicle of the school toilets. Just as I entered the house, I could not help but think that something was out of place.

I could not tell right away, but I knew something was amiss. As I walked purposefully up the stairs, it came to me, it was the smell of good home-cooked food. As I made my way into the bathroom, I wondered at length whether this aroma was indeed in my mind, but on entering the bathroom, things were infinitely clear. I noticed that my sister's panties, the one I used the clean myself after my handy work with the catalogue and The Joy of Sex book, had been taken out of the laundry basket from where I had placed it, or at least where I hoped I had placed it.

I made good my opportunity to clean myself before I went back downstairs to find out if indeed the aroma was coming from our kitchen. I finished in the bathroom and stormed into my room and put on a change of clothes, by now that bounce and skip had all but left me, but I knew I had to go downstairs and investigate this sweet smell of home-cooked food. I looked up at my cloud and, as ever, it was there ever-growing and ever-changing in its form, I ran downstairs and into the kitchen and it was immediately evident that in fact, the aroma was indeed emanating from our very kitchen.

My heart sunk as this could only mean one thing, and that was my mother did have the day off! My mother was not in the house, but I now had cause to fret as my sister's panties, the one I had used to clean myself, could only have been moved by my mother. I thought at length how this could have possibly gone wrong? All at once, the confidence I had previously worn, had suddenly left me, and I was now in a state of damage limitation action. I thought if asked, what could I possibly say about what happened to my sister's panties? I searched my mind, but there was no hint of a constructive reply to such a question.

In earnest, I made my way back upstairs and went into my bedroom, and as usual, laid on my back looking up at my cloud just below the ceiling.

***

Chapter Eight

CAUGHT RED HANDED

'**M**ICHAEL!' I could not tell if I was dreaming or whether it was indeed a reality, I could hear my name being called, but it seemed strangely faint. 'MICHAEL', rang out again but this time it was no longer faint, it was in fact, the sound of my mother calling out to me, for it seemed I had once again drifted off to sleep while laying on my back on my bed looking up at my cloud.

I can say with all certainty that my very fluffy white cloud was no more. 'MICHAEL', I heard ring out once more, 'boy' she said, 'please don't make me have to come up there and show you the slapping side of my hand', and with that, I summarily jumped up and ran downstairs. I arrived in the kitchen to the wondrous smell of home cooking, then I looked down at the dining table and noticed that there were only three places set at the table. I noticed my middle sister had already taken her place at the dinner table, and my mother was standing over the stove dishing out the plates.

Why are there only three places made up at the table? Where are my brother's and big sister's? To this very question, I received no reply. I looked across at my middle sister sitting at the table and she was looking at me in the only way that I can describe as being sideways. I hear you say, 'sideways? What indeed is the very meaning of such a look?' Well, allow me a moment to attempt to try and relate to you the meaning of looking sideways. If then you can imagine for me a time in which you have been in a room, or out in public shopping perhaps, and you are overwhelmed with a sense that eyes are upon you.

In most cases, of course, we tend to shrug them off as nothing more than a fleeting glance, but there are times when one feels eyes are focused upon you, and you turn around sharply, only to find that an individual is looking directly at you, and staring at you from your feet and slowly progressing to your head usually with a crunched up or twisted expression on their face. The lingering stare would only be broken when your two eyes made four, then this was usually followed by a gulping action as if they had just swallowed something very unpleasant.

This then, I hope, will best describe to you the look I was indeed receiving from my sister at the kitchen table. I confess that at that moment I had completely forgotten about all the events of the day, I certainly drifted off into the deepest of sleep when I went upstairs, but at pace, my recall was indeed being reactivated. My mother turned to me and said, 'please sit down to eat because we have an awful lot to talk about'. Suddenly my throat became dry with a sudden loss of appetite. That wonderful smell of home cooking had suddenly left me all the while my sister continued to hold her sideways gaze.

I sensed now that I was in for a grilling and I tried to think fast on my feet and started to think up excuses as to how my sister's panties had been taken off the drying horse and then into such a state. In a flash I had gone through my entire repertoire of possible reasons why the panties were in such a state, it seemed the events of the day had come rushing back to me as if at the speed of light, but nothing and I mean nothing, would prepare me for what was about to come my way.

My mother told me to take my place at the table since the question about my older brother and sister did not have the desired effect. I had hoped that if the whole family were sitting at the table, that would have somehow averted the imminent scolding I was about to receive. I took my place at the table and all the while my middle sister kept her intense gaze. My mother served us our plates and took her place at the table. Being from my particular racial background and being working-class, it was important to say a few words of grace, so I lowered my head in preparation for my mother to say a few words.

A long silence ensued as not a word was said, I started to raise my head ever so slowly only to find my mother and my middle sister still looking at me sideways. I felt a heat rushing from my feet to my head, if I had been from the same racial background as Neola Marton for example, my face would be glowing bright red right by now. Alas then this was not the case, but in my case, it was the presence of sweat, I could feel the beads of sweat gathering on my forehead and also at the end of my nose.

I thought maybe if I kept talking I could perhaps overt the impending onslaught. I said, 'mother you did not say grace, would you like me to say grace?' My mother held her gaze and said, 'you will certainly need to say grace, by the time I'm finished with you'. It was at this moment I knew that I was not going to be able to sweet talk my way out of this, I was now resigned to my plight, and it felt as if life was draining out of me. I looked at my plate of food, the best home cooking you could ever imagine, but my stomach could not face it.

My mother and middle sister dropped their gaze only to start eating heartily, while I still couldn't do anything more but stare at my plate, my mother tells me to 'eat up son or is there something wrong with your food?' I knew what was coming next as I had seen it many times before when my older brother was about to be scolded for the many calamities he had undergone. My mother would always be super calm and enjoyed the meal she had prepared just before she would let rip, my mother asked, 'how was school today?' I could do nothing but stare down at my plate.

I knew I needed to answer and answer quickly, but I found myself as if paralysed, transfixed to the spot. I heard my mother take a breath and I knew if she had to ask the question again, I would surely be in more trouble. Suddenly, it would seem, my ability to speak had returned. 'Well! Well!'. 'Which part of well, has anything to do with the answer to my question?' my mother replied. I tried again to utter something remotely adequate, but yet again, paralysis took over. Mother said, 'ok let me try another question, do you know what happened to the clothes that were drying in your sister's bedroom?'

With this question, I was certain of my undoing. I had better say something, I thought to myself. I used this opportunity to take my fork and pushed some food in my mouth. I remember stuffing at least two forks worth of food in one go. I could scarcely breathe and masticated as though my very life depended on it. I uttered through the mass that had engulfed my mouth, 'umm', it would seem that this little ploy had for the moment worked. Mother said, 'how many times do I have to tell you not to speak with your mouth full?'

As I continued to consume the remainder of the contents in my mouth, I looked up at both my mother and middle sister's cloud and noticed the distinct difference between the two. My mother's cloud was a large shimmering pristine black cloud, which was in complete contrast to that of my middle sister's which was again large but, in her case, fluffy and white. I managed the last morsel of the food in my mouth just in time to check my cloud. 'I thought you were coming to see the musical recital today' I said, I was sure that would mean I was indeed in school.

Mother said, 'so how did you do on stage?' I shoved another fork full of food into my mouth in a bid to buy more time, well again for the time it seemed to be working as I was sure that both my mother and middle sister would finish their dinner before me. I thought if I can just keep this up long enough, I may just wear both my mother and middle sister out. Mother said 'you seem to have a selective memory because the question first asked of you was how was school today?'. A pause of utter silence fell about the kitchen.

The second question was 'do you know what happened to the clothes drying in your sisters' bedroom?' There was nothing left in my mouth to chew, 'I don't know what happened to the clothes in my sister's room' I said. I knew this was a mistake, but I could think of anything better to say, it was like the old code that I was taught by my big brother once you tell a story, you must stick to it. I remembered BLUE is BLUE, and it could never be BLUE is GREEN, that would be a sure way to catastrophe.

Mother said, 'do you happen to know anything about the catalogue or the books on your sister's bookshelf? The catalogue is not in the same place I left it, and for some strange reason, the pages of your sister's books are stuck together'.

Mother said, 'don't tell me you don't know anything about that too?' Well, if there were beads of sweat on my forehead and nose before, I can assure you by now I was awash with sweat. Mother said 'I didn't use any pepper at all in this meal, so why are you sweating so profusely?'.

I had now resigned myself to the notion that it could not get any worse than it was right now, I lifted my head to face check my mother's and my middle sister's face in an attempt to gauge their mood. My middle sister had taken up that sideways look posture once again, and my mother, to all intents and purposes, had the very same expression on her face too. If only the earth would open up and swallow me right now, this horrid wretched ordeal would be swallowed up with me, alas the earth did not assist me in this hour of need.

I said I was drinking some juice and it must have spilt on the books, 'oh really!' mother said, 'so how did you manage to get to the bookcase without passing the clothes that were on the clotheshorse?'. 'Oh, yes I must have spilt the juice on the clothes at the same time'. This time it was my mother and middle sister's turn to pause without a word, my mother and middle sister looked at each other and then turned back to look at me. Mother said 'whatever it was you were drinking could not have been juice, because there is no juice on the market as viscose as that'. I confess at the time for not knowing that viscose meant a fluid that is not thick enough to set but not fluid enough to run like water or juice, for example.

Mother said, 'never mind that for now, I have still not gotten an answer to my question about school and the musical recital', 'how did you do on stage?'. By now I had well and truly given up on the idea of eating the rest of my plate of food. My heart rate soared, and the sweat was pouring off me by now, I looked at my mother's cloud and it would seem that it was shimmering pristine, jet black and bursting with energy.

I glanced at my sister's cloud and there it was, fluffy and white, it just seemed to be there, and did not seem to project any real purpose for being there at all, but fluffy white clouds were always there or at least the sight of one was never too far away. Well, it became perfectly obvious that both my mother and middle sister knew exactly what happened to her panties that were drying in her room. Still, as I mentioned previously, nothing was about to prepare me for what was to come next.

Mother said, 'so you have been in school all day today? Just like you have been in all week', I knew I could and should not hesitate with a reply this time, so I said in the most confident manner. 'Yes, mother I have been in school all day today and all week also'. I noticed that long sideways look from both my mother and sister once again. Mother reached into her pocket and pulled out a crunched-up piece of paper and placed it on the table. Mother said 'can you please read this letter to me as I have not got my reading glasses with me'.

I reached across for the crunched-up piece of paper and set about unfolding it, as I unravelled yet another section of this piece of paper, I could not help but think that it looked in some way familiar. But it was indeed on the final fold that everything became apparent to me, once completely unfolded, it was on school headed notepaper. My heart sunk immediately as this looked very much like my suspension letter, and with all these folds and creases it seemed very much like the one I had hidden in the tree on my way home from school on the day of my suspension. Mother said, 'please read it for me' I could scarcely utter a word and started....

'Dear parent/guardian

This letter is to sadly inform you that your son has been suspended for a full week. If you require a more detailed explanation for the reason for this suspension, please do not hesitate to contact me to arrange a time to discuss the matter in more detail'.

Well, as you can imagine, my whole world had collapsed before me, I was certain that I was going to make this week without being detected. Mother said, 'you can leave the rest of your food and go straight upstairs to your room and stay there, you are grounded indefinitely or at least until I am sure you have learnt your lesson'.

IS IT JUST MY CLOUD

With that final instruction, I left the dinner table and went straight up to my room, as ever I lay on my back looking up at my cloud just below the ceiling, thinking back to the events of the day. I eventually drifted off to sleep.

**

Chapter Nine

RED, GREEN, GOLD AND THE NEIGHBOUR

MANY years had gone by since my suspension. It turned out that one of our neighbours had been taking their dog for a walk in the adventure playground when I slipped the suspension letter inside the tree. Who would have bet on that? The damn busybody made the rest of my school life hell after that. Well, as I have said, I was much older now and had been spending a great proportion of my time exploring my cloud formation and that of others. I spent time trying to find out if other people could see them and, if so, what they thought their clouds meant.

I remember speaking to my big brother on many occasions about his cloud, and I would always be mesmerised by his account. He would take me on a journey of spirituality that would leave me feeling heady. He talked about how your cloud was directly linked to the deepest core of your soul, and he said that it works in harmony with the rhythm of your life. What you see it sees, what you feel it feels and what you love it also loves. He would talk about how empowering and powerful it made him feel. I asked him 'do you have a choice as to which cloud you have?'. His reply was a strange one in so far as he said yes and no, this I found very confusing, but my big brother said, 'as you continue your journey exploring your cloud formation, you will surely understand where I am coming from'.

I noticed more and more that my cloud would merge with other clouds in public places, it was like all those years ago when I was a little boy on the back step with my neighbour or in the park with Katy. Though my cloud is a different colour to what it was back then, merging has always remained consistent; it would also seem that the merging would take on a colour line, that is to say, that fluffy white clouds only merged with other fluffy white clouds. The same would be said for the transitional, translucence and pristine shimmering black clouds and so on.

This then was not the same for which racial group a cloud would attach itself to, and I found this fact very interesting indeed. For example, my middle sister who is certainly cut from the same cloth as me but yet our clouds couldn't be any further apart, my middle sister's fluffy white cloud to my ever-increasingly shimmering pristine black cloud. Now I must acknowledge that my cloud also started as a fluffy white cloud, and here I am embarking on the journey to discover the nature of my cloud and its subsequent transition.

Some months later, after speaking to my brother about his cloud, I remember talking to a guy I met on the estate to the west end of my street. Allow me please to take the necessary opportunity to describe to you the visual virtues of this guy; he often wore on his feet what were called Hush Puppies or, as we sometimes called them, earthman boots. This would often be in a tanned or sandy colour and generally accompanied by a pair of tailored trousers with a stitched hem, to show off the boots to full effect. The torso would be dressed in a long sleeve shirt or a regular T-shirt, and he never failed to top it off with his hat.

His hat was large, woolly and had three very distinct stripes on it. The colours, as I recall them, were red, yellow and I think the last one was green. I'm pretty sure those are the colours because some of my older brother's friends, had hats very similar to his. I digress, to complete his visual appearance, he had very long hair that was in individual plait-like rolls. I have seen hair like that on the heads of most of my big brother's friends. The reason I have gone through such a lengthy description is chiefly because it was very unusual for members of his particular racial background to look and dress like that.

That is to say, he was from the same racial background as Neola Marton, Katy from the adventure playground and even my neighbour from three doors up that I still have such fond memories of. Now, on the other hand, how many people from my particular racial background often looked like him?

Well enough about his description, though I do hope this has at the very least given you a useful mental image to refer to. Months after talking to my brother and meeting this new guy on the estate on the west end of my street, it turned out that he had an amazing story to tell about his cloud and his life in general. He was completely welcoming and seemingly eager to tell me his story. He beckoned me to sit by his side and said, 'I do hope you will have patience with me, in my story about a cloud' he went on to say that 'this cloud is by far no ordinary cloud' in fact he stated, 'this is an incredibly special cloud'.

I took my place at his side on the wall just outside the off-licence. 'Well,' he said, 'to tell you my story about the cloud, I will have to start from the very beginning. It all started when I was a little boy. I was one of eight children which consisted of six boys and two girls. I was the youngest' he said 'when I was a little boy, my older brother and sisters had lots of friends that used to come to the house. They used to drink lots of cans of lager and make lots of noise, this would usually be in the form of shouting and laughter, and they would also play lots of music that sounded as if the people making the music were in some way upset at something because they were always shouting and sounding generally unhappy'. He said that he remembers all his older brothers and their friends had their hair cut short and they used to wear steel toe-capped boots and jeans with green bomber jackets.

This immediately caught my attention as it sounded very much like the description of the gang that set about that boy all those years ago. I did not alert him to that fact as I was very intrigued to hear his account. 'Well, as I have already told you' he said, 'my brothers would make an awful racket most times, but our neighbours never complained'. 'At night, when it was time for me to go to bed, my neighbour would often play a little music, and in my opinion, it was never played loud. I just remember the music as having a real deep baseline and wonderful melodies. I often remember using these musical opportunities to drift off to sleep. As the years went by, I used to look forward to going to bed so that I could be lulled to sleep, by the music that would be played by our neighbour next door'.

He said it was at these moments when going off to sleep that he first noticed his cloud, he used to lay on his back, listening to the music from next-door and look up at his cloud. At first, he thought he could not believe his own eyes as there was this fluffy white cloud just below the ceiling. Wow! I thought that was just like how I used to see my cloud in my early days. He continued his account and talked about when he became a little older, he would hear his big brother and his friends talk about attacking and beating up people, he used to call them a particular name, Rackies, or Lackies, it was something like that. He used to try and get him to join in with the laughter and banter, but for some reason, he was in no way impressed with what they were up to.

He went on to talk about his cloud and how it first started as a fluffy white cloud, but later he noticed it gradually started changing into the form it has today. He seemed not to be too willing to talk any more about his brother and his friends, and the fact that they would often return to his home with stories of bashing some poor soul to a pulp.

Instead, he went on to talk about the relationship he had with his neighbours and the music he would listen to through the walls at night. He said he could not help but think that the music had in some way affected how his cloud had developed. His brothers or sister would come in the house with their friends, and the whole house would be awash with fluffy white clouds. The clouds would be merging with each other and forming, what he would describe as, a super cloud notwithstanding the fact that a super cloud could only be a shimmering pristine black cloud.

'But I will explain that in a little more detail later' he said, he continued to talk about how each night his neighbour would play music, and he would notice a change in his cloud, he also talked about how the beat, rhythm and baseline used to captivate him. He said he remembers one night asking his brother if he could hear the beat of the music coming from next door, his brother would always reply with a rant and call the neighbours nasty names, 'never really could understand all the hate my brothers and sisters had for other people' he said. I asked him to explain what he meant by the neighbour's music having an effect on how his cloud had turned out, and it seemed he was more than delighted to share his account.

He went on to say that every time the music from next door was played, he would find himself completely immersed and in a state of trance within it. He talked about 'feeling vibrations from within, almost spiritual'. He said, 'you must know the music I am talking about', I said 'why so', 'well' he replied, by saying that his neighbours shared the same racial background as me he was sure I, at least, had an idea of the music he was describing. I knew only too well the music he was describing as my older brother and his friends would always be playing music of that type when they came over to our house.

In those days, everybody used to bring their new records to a mutual friend's house, and we would listen to them one after the other, so I was indeed familiar with the music form he was describing and its power to completely draw you in. He went on to say that when he was younger and had a fluffy white cloud, and when he was in the house with the rest of his family, his cloud used to merge with other members of his family. But now since his cloud had taken on an entirely new form, the clouds would never merge, he said this used to be a real point of contention to his mind. He recounted the fact that when his cloud was going through the changing process, it used to change from the fluffy white cloud into a putrid off white and then to greyish off white.

He said that it was very alarming to him, I can recall the moment when my cloud started to change from the fluffy white cloud to the putrid off-white and then to a greyish off-white cloud. It was at the moment of my betrayal in the Headmaster's office with Neola Marton that I too had a moment of concern at the change in the composition of my cloud all those years ago. It would, therefore, seem that our clouds are in some way linked to our physical, mental and/or emotional state. I bade him to continue with his account, which I must say I found most fascinating. He went on to say that he would often stop and talk to his neighbour whenever he came home and saw his neighbour working in his garden He said that he would often be invited into his neighbour's home to have some tea and a slice of cake.

He said the thing he noticed the most about being in his neighbour's home was the immense size and colour of his neighbour's cloud; he went on to say that he thought his neighbour's cloud was perfect in every sense of the word. He described his neighbour's cloud as being completely black, with immense size and shimmering with awesome power and in pristine condition. As he spoke to his neighbour about life in general, he found that his cloud would take on some of the characteristics of his neighbour's cloud, this coupled with the reaction to the music he would hear through the wall at bedtime also added to the change.

Since he mentioned my racial background and the fact that he thought that I should be aware of the music he had been describing, I thought I would take the opportunity to ask him a question relating to his racial background. Then I said, 'it is indeed very unusual for members of your racial background to dress in the way you do, and it is even rarer for members of your racial background to have such an amazing shimmering pristine black cloud'. It was at this point that he stopped me in my tracks and said, 'what exactly do you mean by members of my racial background not dressing or having the same cloud formation as members of your racial background?' I stuttered and said 'well', but before I could utter another word, he said, 'I got you! I had you all over the ropes with that one!'.

'That one caught you just like a phantom punch' he exclaimed laughing from his stomach all the while, and he said, 'I am going to tell you a little story about race and the fact that race does not have a place in this world, but sadly it would seem race has taken centre stage on the world we live in today'. He talked in the most spiritual form, and I was truly captivated by his account and his apparent abundance of knowledge and wisdom, everything he said linked everything together and was not disjointed compared to the traditional learning methods. He went on to say 'I am going to tell you a little bit about my ancestors. In the Fifteenth and Sixteenth Centuries, my ancestors did a lot of global circumnavigation'.

This circumnavigation gave way to massive claims of newly discovered lands and stories of wealth in terms of natural resources and things of that description. The thing he said that indeed he found strange about the claims his ancestors would make was the fact that each and every place his ancestors would "discover" would already have people living there. This was a subject I heard my older brother talking about with his friends in our house. I was fascinated to hear a person from his racial background speaking about this very subject. He went on to say that while his ancestors were landing in new territories, discovering new plants they would be used for medicine or sugars, as well as a raft of other natural resources that were to be used to develop the part of the world his ancestors "originated" from.

I bade him to continue with his account for which he was more than obliging. So he said 'his ancestors noticed that with each landing they made, they would find the people they encountered having a similarity to each other, but no similarity to his landing ancestors'. I was riveted by his openness and honesty, as in my experience, it was not at all common for people who shared the same racial background as him to speak in such a way about their history. I was transfixed as he continued to explain that after his exploring ancestors returned from a journey, they would inform their royal and noble commissioners of the fact that there was no one anywhere in the known world similar to his ancestors.

This by itself should not be an opportunity for a lengthy debate, but it would seem sparked off the beginnings of the concept of racial classification. Before this time he said, 'you would have been known as the people of the waterfall if your village was settled near to a waterfall. The same would be said for people living close to an active volcano, as they could have been known as the people of the smoking mountain and so on. Then, as I said when my ancestors realised that there were in fact no other people on the known planet that looked like them, this led the royals and noblemen who commissioned the voyages to perceive a reason for alarm'. He went on to say that he still had not worked out if the concern of his ancestors had been in any way founded, but he was certain that the effects of having a racial classification of people have no doubt taken centre stage in the world that we live in today.

I asked him to tell me a little bit about how his shimmering pristine black cloud made him feel? He looked at me and chuckled and said, 'you mock me my newly found friend', he exclaimed 'you know very well the feeling of having a shimmering pristine black cloud'. I had to admit he wore his cloud exceptionally well, he was truly in tune with his cloud, and it would seem his cloud was completely in tune with him. I said, 'this should not stop you from expressing to me how your cloud makes you feel', he again looked at me and smiled saying 'you are indeed right it should not, and it will not stop me from telling you how my shimmering pristine black cloud makes me feel'.

He said once he had decided to embrace the change in his cloud, which he noticed while growing up, he said it was a very easy choice. He knew he had found something in the vibrations of the music that used to seep through his bedroom wall at night, but he also said that he was so taken by the spirituality of his neighbour that it also made it an easy decision to be content with the new form his cloud had taken. It seemed to me that he had a great level of respect for the man that lived next door to him, he went on to say that if he can only be a fraction of the man his neighbour was, he was sure that he would shine a great light on to this universe. I thought that to be a very nice thing to say about a person, to be inspired in that way was truly amazing.

I asked him about the clouds of the rest of his family and why he did not take on the characteristics of his immediate family? His reply was swift and to the point. He exclaimed that the cloud formation that would be found in his home was the formation of indifference, he said that he did not see much spirituality within it and it would seem would too often skirt around the truth. In other words, he said that when he was in the presence of mass fluffy white cloud formations, there seemed to be a need to find a group, any group, that was in some way different and ridicule them in some way. This could simply be someone on television, for example, as long as they did not have a fluffy white cloud above them or even if they did but was from a different racial background from his family then they would be up for ridicule. He went on to say that he found this lack of spirituality to be a great shame, as he believed that his family were truly missing out on being at one with the universe they lived in.

So I pressed him again to tell me about the feeling he gets from having a shimmering pristine black cloud, he rolled his eyes and said, 'sorry for getting carried away with my family'. I said, 'no apology needed as it was I that asked you to speak about the cloud formation of your family', so he went on to say, 'having the privilege of having a shimmering pristine black cloud was truly an honour'. He also said that 'he believed that social conditioning was responsible for allocating your first cloud to you, they are the things that socialised you the most when you first appeared on this planet'. He said, 'it could be from the things that you were taught by your parents and family, and mass media would also play a massive role in shaping your thoughts and therefore the allocation of your first cloud'.

This, he went on to say, was not in any way set in stone as his cloud proved to have been shaped by the influence of the music that seeped through his walls at night and also my feelings of betrayal in the Headmaster's office with Neola Marton. He said his cloud filled him with confidence and inner peace that seemed to be directly connected or plugged into the universe as he put it, he felt in touch with all that was around him. He said that having a shimmering pristine black cloud seemed to give him the ability to feel the feelings of others and that he said this was in his opinion directly linked to the powerful lessons he had received from his next-door neighbour.

He summed up by saying that his shimmering pristine black cloud gave him an assured confidence, but not confidence that should be mistaken for being deemed over-confident. He also said that he could not bear thinking of life without his shimmering pristine black cloud. With that, I bade him a very warm and good night, and we both got up from the wall in unison and walked off in the direction of our homes. I could not help but turn around to take one more final look at my newly discovered friend. It was as though a connection had been linked between us because as I turned to get one more glance at him, it seemed that he was compelled to do the same, we gave each other a warm smile and continued to walk home.

As I got to the top of the path that led to my house, I could hear the sound of happy voices coming from inside, I figured that it was my older siblings minus my middle sister having a house party or a drink up for one of their friend's birthdays. I remembered pushing the key in the door and entering and not being noticed by anyone, so I went straight upstairs to the bedroom that I still shared with my older brother, and I laid down on my back looking up at my cloud hovering just above the ceiling. I guess you know what happened next, just like each and every time before, I drifted off into a deep and restful sleep.

MICHAEL J. CHARLES

***

Chapter Ten

SHETITA

TIME had again passed since I chatted with the guy with the red, yellow and green hat. I remembered being so moved and influenced by his account of his cloud that after speaking with him, I remembered taking the time to study global circumnavigation in the Fifteenth and Sixteenth Centuries, and the advent of global racial classification that seemed to spawn therefrom. I had indeed found a great many claims of discovery of newly found lands, and stories of the bounties that would be found in those new lands. I too, just like my older brother and the guy with the red, yellow and green hat, noticed that these discoveries were being made in lands that already had native populations and, in fact, had populations there for millennia.

It was also true what the guy with the red, yellow and green hat said about his ancestors and the fact that on each and every landing they did not encounter any people who looked like them. I tried to put myself in the shoes of one of his ancestors and wondered what it must have been like to set off, to make an eastern or easterly discovery, only to find oneself in a west or westerly landmass. As expected, he harboured little hope that he may indeed discover a landmass with people that looked in some way the same as he did only to find, yet again, a landmass that had populations living there already and still for over millennia.

I wondered what it must have been like to have landed in one of those places and then witness the sight of a mass of shimmering pristine black clouds. It must have been as close to an image of a place known as heaven. Let me take a necessary moment to explain to you the definition of heaven as the most commonly used thesaurus would dictate. Heaven is a place of paradise, bliss, ecstasy, rapture and/or a dreamland, to mention but a few descriptions. It was indeed true that there was, in fact, only one group of people that shared virtually all the characteristics of all the other so-called discovered peoples, but the one thing that remained unique about this group was their cloud formation.

The cloud formation of this one group corresponded directly to the group of people that were often singled out for beatings from the group of boys that would wear steel toe-capped boots, have short hair and green bomber jackets. I remember vividly that the guy who took such a horrific beating by the River Brent at the back of my house and the adventure playground, had a cloud formation, but the cloud did not have any colouration. That is to say, there was indeed a cloud over this poor guy, but

I remember distinctly noticing that his cloud was translucent with no filling whatsoever.

I remember when I noticed it at school on the day I snuck into school while being suspended for having the best morning's pelvic workout imaginable. I have not gotten over the fact that I was suspended all those years ago and that feeling of being betrayed. I also remember noticing that same cloud formation as that poor guy that had been set upon. I remember getting the opportunity to speak to one of these people, and I must say they rarely made conversation an easy aspect of human interaction and activity. I found talking to them incredibly strained and laborious, it would seem to me at least, but an opportunity had indeed presented itself, so I made the best use of the time offered to me.

I remember standing up while Shetita sat on the ground crossed legged; I remember her having to squint up as the sun was high in the sky and directly behind me at the time. Shetita said 'I understand you want to ask me a question', 'well' I replied, 'as a matter fact I do have a couple of questions I would like to ask you'. I said, 'the questions are related to your particular racial group and background'. I could not help but notice a perplexed look on her face when I mentioned the words race and background. Bearing in mind, I have this same conversation with many other people from racially diverse backgrounds and, though some among them may have been a little guarded at first, I never got the impression that question was a perplexing one.

Shetita beckoned me to sit beside her. Well, I must say this was most unusual, as most of the time people from her particular racial background would never want to be seen talking to a boy, and particularly a boy from a different racial background as herself. I admit to being taken by surprise at this invitation and looked around to see if there was anybody who I thought could maybe make her change her mind as I must also add that she was an incredibly attractive girl. Many girls from her particular racial background appeared to be very attractive to look at, so I made good the offer afforded to me.

I sat down beside Shetita and said, 'though I mentioned your racial group and your background, the question was more in fact about your cloud and the clouds of most of the people who shared the same racial background as you'. Again, I noticed the perplexed look return to her face, but this time I could not help but ask why her face had adopted such a perplexed look? Shetita replied by saying, 'my face is like this because from an early age I have been taught to ignore my cloud'. I wondered at length what could be the purpose of ignoring something so fundamental to people who shared this planet. I asked, 'who was it that would tell you such a thing?'.

Shetita gave out a long sigh and said, 'it starts right from the first time your cloud appears', she said she remembered the first time her cloud appeared. She remembered it as vividly as if it were yesterday, she talked about going to bed one night, and she recalled that she was around four or five years old. She remembered lying on her back in bed and seeing, just below the ceiling, a most amazing shimmering pristine black cloud. She said she was utterly taken aback by its majestic presence and felt totally at one with it appearing; she remembered drifting off to sleep that night with complete excitement in wanting to tell her mother about what she had seen hovering just below the ceiling in her bedroom the night before.

Shetita said she awoke the next morning to the sound of birds chirping and the sun wanting to penetrate through the blinds. She got out of bed that morning and immediately ran downstairs. Shetita admitted to not even taking much time to wash her face or brush her teeth. She said she was awash with excitement at the prospect of telling her mother and father the story of the cloud she had seen the night before. 'Mother', 'Father' she said as she was rushing into the kitchen. She was running so fast she nearly knocked the contents of her father's breakfast out of her mother's hand. Her mother said, 'whatever is the matter, why are you running around like a wild animal?'.

Shetita took her place at the breakfast table and could barely contain herself; she was simply bursting with excitement to tell her parents about her cloud. She said 'mum, dad last night just before I fell asleep, just below the ceiling in my bedroom was a beautiful, shimmering pristine black cloud, it was amazing!'.

She went on to say that it felt like a shield had arrived to protect her through life. Shetita's mother and father sat in silence and simply stared at each other. Shetita quickly realised that something was not quite right, but she did not have the benefit of experience to help her understand what the exact problem was.

She continued to say that the cloud came as if from nowhere and simply appeared above her head, she said that there was nothing alarming about the cloud at all. The cloud seemed to be able to connect directly to her inner self and emitted spiritual energy, which seemed to penetrate to her deepest core. Shetita looked up at her parents and noticed her father nodding to her mother, as if to say, 'tell her'. Shetita's father was nodding in her direction, and her mother seemed to be reluctant to speak, but finally, it seemed Shetita's mother regained the ability to speak and said 'Shetita darling you know both your mother and father love you, don't you?'.

As I have already said, she was a little girl at the time and had very little life experience to draw from, Shetita replied, 'yes mother I know you both love me very much'. So, her mother went on to say, 'I have to speak to you about the cloud you saw last night'. Shetita said that a feeling of excitement had returned to her as she was very eager to talk about her shimmering pristine black cloud. 'Mummy' she said, 'I have witnessed the most amazing cloud that I think has been sent to be my protector for life', her mother replied by saying 'my darling you have got to try and forget that cloud you have seen'.

Shetita said her heart sunk at the very notion of having to learn to forget her newly found companion, and she asked her mother why she should start to forget her cloud? Shetita's mother attempted to explain the very complicated reason that her daughter should try to forget about the shimmering pristine black cloud that had recently entered her life. Her mother said that the shimmering pristine black cloud that she had seen came from the souls of the original ancestors who started humanity, even though Shetita was very young, she was confident enough to say that must have been a good thing. Shetita said 'that must be the reason why my cloud felt like it was here to protect me' again a silence had overtaken the kitchen once more.

Shetita's mother went on to say that it would be better if Shetita focused on the people who had fluffy white clouds. The reason for this was because the original ancestors of humanity are now thought of as being primitive. Shetita's mother said, 'we are in a new country now, and we should not have anything to do with those we originated from'. Shetita was very confused with the answer she had been given, but she understood the idea of not being considered as being primitive, but for many years Shetita said her shimmering pristine black cloud continued to visit her. She remembered being caught between the sound of her mother's voice resonating in her head, and the total tranquillity her cloud would emit on each and every occasion it appeared.

Shetita had become much older by now and had sadly become used to ignoring her visiting cloud and instead spent an awful lot of time observing the people her mother had told her to observe. The more Shetita observed the people who had fluffy white clouds, the more her cloud seemed to lose its sense of colour and energy. As the years passed, Shetita found that the people who had fluffy white clouds, often stayed in their own groups and were not at all welcoming, she noticed that although not all people with fluffy white clouds shared the same racial background as each other, their characteristics all seemed to be the same. That is to say that they used to form groups that had subdivisions within it, the most common thing was that they always seemed to be spending time either pointing out the faults of others or subdividing themselves into even more divided groups.

Shetita noticed that the fluffy white clouds of all the different racial groups still merged together to make super large cloud formations. She never felt that the fluffy white clouds had any mystical, spiritual or magical elements to it and observed that the fluffy white clouds just seemed to be there and look rather pretty without having any particular use. Shetita said that on no occasion while speaking to one of the people with fluffy white clouds did she feel any sense of spirituality. She went on to say that in fact, she never seemed to find a sense of wisdom from them, having a fluffy white cloud seemed to be superficial and devoid of purpose.

But this was very hard for Shetita to accept as she knew very well that the cloud that she had been told to ignore, did indeed have a multitude of energies present that inspired, empowered, protected and nurtured all that accepted it. Shetita was sure she did not want to have a fluffy white cloud, but she had so much fear and respect for her mother and father that she learnt to ignore her shimmering pristine black cloud. The result of which left her with a colourless cloud that is neither fluffy and white or shimmering pristine black, or any of the other shades between those colours. Shetita said that to please her family, she had to deny her feelings, and each time she ignored her original cloud, the more she felt she had lost a piece of her essence.

I was stunned by what I had just heard, I know I had asked the question why people who shared the same racial background as Shetita had cloud formations which had no colouration, but in truth, nothing could have prepared me for the account I had just heard. Shetita then turned and looked at me and said, 'now do you understand why people from my racial background behave in the way we do?'. Shetita went on to say that even when we came home and told our parents that the people with fluffy white clouds often singled them out, the net result of being singled out was either to be on the end of verbal abuse, or worse still be at the receiving end of a severe beating.

I could not help but think back to the guy who received a severe beating at the hands of the steel toe-capped wearing gang all those years ago, Shetita and the guy that was set upon were from the same racial background as each other. I noticed a tear rolling down her face, and I was filled with a sense of helplessness because I didn't know what to do. On the one hand, I wanted to reach over and comfort and console her, but on the other hand, social conditioning made me freeze with fear as to the consequence Shetita might have to face from her parents if we were indeed seen in an embrace.

I could not contain myself anymore as I turned towards Shetita with outstretched arms, and she turned toward me and sunk into my embrace. I have to, at this time, confess to the rapid beat of my heart at that very moment, I now, in fact, had two emotions running concurrently, on the one hand, I was concerned at her apparent emotional state and the other the prospect of embracing Shetita. Well, it would seem that the latter had taken centre stage; I embraced her very tightly and began to stroke her arms, neck and shoulders. I noticed that she did not react negatively, so my stroking became all the more sensual, Shetita turned and looked at me, and I was sure she was about to object to my physical advances.

To my utter and total surprise, she did not object. Shetita turned to me and gave me what I could only describe as being the very best French kiss I had ever had the pleasure of experiencing. I could barely contain myself, my pulse rate had, I believe, at least tripled, and my forehead had several beads of sweat trickling from it. Shetita suddenly pulled away and got up and thanked me for being interested in her cloud formation, her final words as she bade me goodbye were, 'I hope you may have a greater understanding of why people who share the same racial background as I have clouds without any colouration'.

With that, Shetita walked off in the direction of her home. I sat in the same spot and looked on at her as she walked into the distance. I must confess that Shetita was very much like Neola Marton; in as far as her physical form took on the characteristics of women that came from my racial background. As she walked into the distance, I was caught between the amazing account she had just given me about why her cloud and the clouds of a large proportion of her racial group were the way they were. The other thing I was indeed occupied with was the amazing French kiss I had just had the pleasure of experiencing. I wondered indeed if Shetita could ever become the new Neola Marton.

After I sat in the same spot for a while, I made my way home feeling content that I had just learnt a very valuable lesson in as far as I had finally found a possible reason why the cloud of the guy who had been set upon all those years ago lacked any colouration within a cloud. It was primarily brought on by social conditioning, which can be administered from members of your own family, teachers, and/or the mass media. I got home and went straight to my bedroom, and like each and every other time I had an encounter relating to my cloud or the clouds of others, I laid on my back and looked up at the ceiling to admire my shimmering pristine black cloud and drifted off to sleep.

***

Chapter Eleven

SOCIAL GROUPS

LONG after Shetita's account, I found myself looking even deeper into the concept of social conditioning. I was also convinced that there might be a link between what the guy with the red, yellow and green hat said about his ancestors and revisited information I found on the Fifteenth and Sixteenth Centuries.

It was indeed true that several studies and books were written about the classification of human beings. Prior to this new era, people were identified based on a variety of things; these would typically include things that the people could identify with. For example, as I mentioned in an earlier chapter, if you and the people you were associated with lived beside a stream, it was entirely possible that you may have been known as the people of the stream. Conversely, if you came from a people that were settled close to an active volcano, again it would be entirely possible that you could have been known as the people of the smoking mountain. During the era of global circumnavigation carried out by the ancestors of the guy with the red, yellow and green hat, it seems there became a need to change the classification of people.

The new classification would no longer take into consideration the location, cultural, spiritual or work ethics of those people. In fact, all the natural environmental indicators of what people could be called were now to be turned on its head. The global circumnavigators decided on a new classification that would only consider the climate, features and skin tone of the people, for example by the Seventeenth Century, books that were described as scientific were being published about racial classification.

In Seventeen Hundred and Thirty-Five Carl Linnaeus published a work called 'A General System of Nature', in this work he talked, amongst other things, about being able to put people into groups. He was, as it would seem, trying to create a hierarchy of human beings and stated that people could be classified by cultural and climatic differences. He went on to say that people can then be divided into four distinct sub-categories, and I shall quote them as I found them:

1. **AMERICANUS.** Native American males were supposedly red; had black hair and sparse beards; were stubborn; prone to anger; "free"; and governed by traditions. Thus, this form of *homo sapiens* was inferior and uncivilized.

2. **ASIATICUS**. The male Asian was said to be "yellowish, melancholy, endowed with black hair and brown eyes, severe, conceited, and stingy. He puts on loose clothing. He is governed by opinion". Thus, like the aforementioned type of *homo sapiens*, the *Asiaticus* could only be a mediocre prototype.

3. **AFRICANUS**. The male of this subset, according to Linnaeus, could be recognized by his skin tone, face structure, and curly hair. This kind was apparently cunning, passive, and inattentive, and ruled by impulse. The female of this kind was also apparently shameless, because "they lactate profusely".

4. **EUROPEAUS**. The males of this subset were supposedly "changeable, clever, and inventive. He puts on tight clothing. He is governed by laws".

Though I have used only one example of people who were developing systems to classify the populations of the world, it struck me that in fact, only 1/10th of the world's population were developing systems that would classify the remaining 9/10th of the world's population. The question for me was why would there be a need for such a classification in the first place? I pondered on the idea for some time, but an answer has not been forthcoming to this point.

I examined the idea of whether the classification of people could influence what cloud you were first given? Or could the knowledge of the classification of people change the cloud formation that you were first given? I remember, quite vividly, my fluffy white cloud as a young boy, but I also remember the precise moment in which the change came about to my fluffy white cloud. Though I had up to that point thought that all fluffy white clouds merged when near each other, I remember being completely shocked when Neola Marton's cloud merged with the Headmaster's all those years ago, but my cloud remained isolated.

From that moment on, my cloud never merged with Neola Marton's, I would be nothing short of a liar if I said that even after the ordeal in the Headmaster's office, her physical form was still that of the highest ilk, but from the moment my fluffy white cloud began its transformation, it seemed to react in unison to my emotions at that time; and the feeling of utter betrayal. Something from deep inside had changed, and I remember how upset I felt at the Headmaster treating Neola Marton as a victim, which incidentally was the farthest thing from the truth. Truth, now there's a funny word, truth - Neola Marton positively lapped up the idea of being the victim.

But if you had the same privilege as me to have had Neola Marton in the same year as you in school, you would indeed know that Neola Marton took her sexual pleasures very seriously indeed. She was most forthcoming once you had the pleasure of being her choice, which made me feel all the more betrayed in the Headmaster's office. Another time which brought about another significant change to my fluffy white cloud was witnessing the beating of that guy all those years ago by the steel toe-capped green bomber jacket wearing gang.

I remember those moments bringing about a massive change in the appearance of my fluffy white cloud, this coupled with listening to the account of my older brother and his friends, and each day it would seem a little more change would occur. I thought so much about the cloud of the guy who took the beating all those years ago and also what I had learnt from Shetita. I remember noticing the guy's cloud rather late on that day down by the river, he had the same cloud formation as Shetita and shared the same racial background as her. I thought at length how hard it must have been for him to be set upon by a gang of boys, who were sporting the very cloud he would have been socially conditioned by his parents to imitate.

Now I have gained a little further knowledge about the clouds we all have, I wondered why his cloud never changed to a fluffy white cloud or remained a shimmering pristine black cloud. I pondered on this thought for some time and I came up with the notion based on what I had learnt from Shetita, that perhaps it was the pressure from their parents not to accept the shimmering pristine black cloud they were born with, and the pressure they must feel for having to adopt the fluffy white cloud of the people who would often both physically and verbally abuse them.

The adage, caught between a rock and a hard place, comes to mind. It must have been truly soul-destroying to be conditioned to ignore the cloud you were born with, only to accept a cloud of those that show such intolerance by many of the people who sported them. It was even stranger in fact that not everybody with a fluffy white cloud was of the same racial background, but for whatever reason, the guy who suffered the beating by the river and Shetita never took on a cloud with any colouration at all. I thought back to all the things Shetita told me about her cloud and the social conditioning from her parents to teach her to do what did not feel at all natural to her.

I could not help but think that it must be the hardest thing ever to live in this world without the choice of a cloud. I spent some time learning about clouds, their composition and formations, in the hope of finding out about their role on this planet, and ultimately their purpose in our lives. I was amazed to discover that clouds had specific names, and even contained immense energy and power. For example, you have ten individual cloud names. I shall list them and their functions while paying special focus to the clouds that are most mentioned in this book.

Well, as I have mentioned, I will list the names of these clouds, and indeed I shall start as ever with the fluffy white clouds, though I must confess to not having a single motive for listing it in this way:

1. **CIRRUS** clouds form when the wind blows these ice crystals into wispy streaks that look like thin horsetails.

2. **CIRROCUMULUS** clouds look like upside-down waves rolling across the sky.

3. High, thin **CIRROSTRATUS** clouds look much like stratus clouds, but cirrostratus clouds contain ice crystals and are much higher.

4. **ALTOCUMULUS** clouds look fleecy and have dark, shadowed sides.

5. **ALTOSTRATUS** clouds are flat and make the sun look as if it is being seen through a misty glass.

6. **CUMULONIMBUS** clouds are piled up high like scoops of dark ice cream. These clouds usually bring rain showers.

7. **STRATOCUMULUS** clouds are spread out heaps of dense cover that rise higher in the atmosphere.

8. Dark, flat **NIMBOSTRATUS** clouds often produce rain or snow.

9. **CUMULUS** clouds look like giant heads of cauliflower because they are white and fluffy.

10. **STRATUS** clouds are spread out, dull clouds usually found at ground level. Stratus clouds may be so close to the ground they are identified as fog.

Now we have listed the names of the clouds, I also may point to the fact that the scientific rationale can be found in any self-respecting library. I shall attempt to give you a rationale sometimes found among more common man.

It is often said by people describing the weather conditions of any given day that say something like this.... 'Oh! today is going to be a lovely day, because the sky is blue with fluffy white clouds' for example. You may also hear something like this, 'Oh! today is going to be a dull day because the clouds are grey', need I continue and describe what is said about a day that is filled with black clouds?

I shall indeed inform you as to what is said on a day filled with black clouds. It is often said that 'today is going to be a bad day because the clouds are black'. Well, I could not help relating that idea to people and in particular to the colouration of their clouds. Is it then true? Or could it be true that the same classifications can be made about people? That is to say, all people who sport a fluffy white cloud are good and happy people? And conversely, people with greyish clouds are both good and bad?

I was now left with a real dilemma. I now had to ask the question does this mean that people with pristine shimmering black clouds are bad and sad? To answer these questions, I needed to embark on forming my own analysis of what cloud classification meant to me, so I pondered on the notion of fluffy white clouds nestled in a lush blue sky.

There could be no doubt that such a day could only be described as a good day, for example, the idea of being able to wear a pair of sandals, a marina or a nice baggy T-shirt. On days such as these, you could also find the sights of a range of fine women sporting cut down shorts and backless tops, all of which added to giving the day an extra feel-good factor. The question for me though ran a little deeper than just simply a feel-good factor, the question for me was, what impact, if any, did/do fluffy white clouds have on the earth and/or the perpetuation or the replenishment thereof?

It struck me for a moment that even on days where the sky is blue, with very little fluffy white clouds in the sky, the sun was still able to feed the earth with light that helps in the growth of our produce. It also helps with warming up the blood of cold-blooded animals, for example. But on a day when there is a lot of fluffy white clouds, though they may look attractive in the sky, they often impede the sun from penetrating through them and feeding the plants and warming up the many cold-blooded animals and creatures that rely on it.

This then left me with a problem. The problem being that, why were the days that had fluffy white clouds described as being good days, when in fact, with very little probing, it could be argued that fluffy white clouds may look good, but in fact, can impede valuable processes the earth and animals need to meet their full potential? I then turned to the question of a day with greyish clouds, and the idea that a day such as this meant that it could be a good or bad day. The thing was my take on this again was different, I found that a day with greyish clouds indicated that the earth was about to be replenished in as far as it meant that the time of the pristine shimmering black cloud was about to appear.

Pristine shimmering black clouds. I must say that they are not very often described in this way, that is to say, pristine shimmering and black. A day with pristine shimmering black clouds is often described as bad and sad days. But here was the thing, when looking up the scientific definition, I found that pristine shimmering black clouds are described as being powerful, a fact I did not know up to that point.

Take for example the Cumulonimbus or the Nimbostratus clouds, clouds such as these are often regarded as dark gloomy and/or bleak clouds, but is that really true? With further inspection, one may find that those clouds are the complete opposite of that which can be described as gloomy or bleak. I am led to believe that at least eighty percent of the earth is covered in water, the same too I understand is the case with man who is eighty percent made of fluid. In most cases, with the absence of water, the earth finds it hard to replenish itself. This then is where Cumulonimbus and the Nimbostratus clouds come into their own.

Both of these clouds contain immense powers, one of which is the vital rain that all life forms require for survival, some of those clouds even hold immense electrical powers in the shape of lighting. That then is the very point I am trying to make, if these pristine shimmering black clouds hold so much goodness needed to replenish the earth, why then are they described in such a negative light? As I have previously mentioned, a common view of dark/black clouds is that of bad luck, gloom, washout, dark, just to mention a few. But here is the thing, for me, the arrival of the pristine shimmering black clouds, signifies new life, and the washing away of dead and fallen life.

I truly find it hard to see pristine shimmering black clouds as anything other than life-giving. Conversely, when one talks about fluffy white clouds, the tone always seems to take on a happy or magical tone. That is to say, today the sky is blue, filled with fluffy white clouds; therefore, today is going to be a good day. But I can't help but think back to the description given by the guy wearing the red, yellow and green hat. He described a day with the sky filled with fluffy white clouds in a different way. He went on to say that a sky filled with fluffy white clouds in his opinion distorted the beauty of the blue canvas in the background.

He talked about a particular day in which he sat basking in the sun, and he remembered sitting under a blue sky filled with fluffy white clouds, and the fact that he drifted off to sleep. But when he awoke and looked up at the sky, he recalled a sky completely devoid of fluffy white clouds. He went on to say that he had never witnessed anything as beautiful as that perfect blue sky, the very thought of a fluffy white cloud in the sky would have completely ruined the spectacle. I could not help but wonder if people thought of our clouds in the same way?

That is to say, are people who sport pristine shimmering black clouds dark, gloomy, bleak and so on? And those with fluffy white clouds as happy, fun, or good? Well, I offer this question to you just for a moment. It struck me that one could not make the same judgments relating to the clouds that we humans sport, the sheer fact that the clouds seemed to choose you at first but, the more one acquired knowledge it would seem that this could influence the type of cloud you may end up with. As you would remember from some of my earlier accounts, about the various people sporting clouds, seemed to cross cultural and racial lines. That is to say that people who shared the same cultural and racial background as me could have completely different clouds.

For example, take my middle sister and I, we are both cut from the same cloth, but we did not share the same colour cloud. My sister sported a large fluffy white cloud, oh! and how very proud of her cloud she was, even though my sister did not have the same trait as the bomber jacket wearing gang. But I still found my sister to be very clinical at best, that for example, my sister could quite easily know someone quite dear to her who was sleeping rough outdoors and this would have very little emotional effect on her, if at all. It seemed to me that many people who supported fluffy white clouds could switch on an air of insensitivity at will, this in my experience was the complete opposite to those sporting pristine shimmering black clouds.

Those with pristine shimmering black clouds always seemed to be very intuitive and/or incredibly sensitive, all of which I recognise in myself, but I wondered just what others might make of it. So, I remembered one early evening my big brother arrived home, he as I have said, had been sporting a pristine shimmering black cloud for many years now, I felt compelled to ask for his views on the subject, that is to say, did he notice if people could be categorised whether or not they were sporting different clouds. To my utter amazement, my older brother exclaimed, 'you have no idea how long I have been waiting for you to ask me a question like that'. So my older brother and I put the kettle on and set the scene for a long and meaningful discussion on clouds, human clouds, and their symbolic significance.

***

Chapter Twelve

CHOICE

THE kettle had just come to the boiling point and my brother reached for a small tin from the top shelf in the kitchen. I thought to myself, that is not where the tea or coffee would be found, but my brother returned to the table with a warm smile on his face. He said 'Michael, you have not tasted anything like this before', to which I replied, 'what do you mean, I haven't had tea or coffee before?' This only made my brother's warm smile turn into a huge roar of laughter. No! he exclaimed, 'this is a special herb tea', giving me a wink at the same time. I must confess that at the time I had no idea of just how good that herb tea would turn out to be but, suffice to say, we sat and began our discussion on the differences between human clouds.

My brother handed me a cup, and almost immediately as the cup was put in front of me, I could smell the aroma of this all too new herbal tea. I can't much describe the smell of this aroma, but I felt pretty sure I had come across it before. My brother takes his seat beside me - you may indeed remember that my mother was famous in our street for making exceptionally good cakes and ice lollies - well need I say that on this very occasion my brother slides over a saucer towards me, containing a large slice of my mother's special rum-soaked cake. These cakes, I must take a moment to describe for you, this type of cake would normally take a year to be produced, a year I hear some of you exclaim! How does any cake take a whole year to be produced? Well, I shall ease your unsolicited agitated state.

This cake is made up of sultanas and raisins as the fruity element of the cake, but the thing is these sultanas and raisins have to be soaked in overproof rum that would normally be brought into the UK by someone either visiting the UK from the Caribbean, or the other way around. I remember my brother saying to me, 'so what is it you are so hell-bent on talking to me about?'. I remember taking a sip of my hot herbal tea then a handsome bite of the cake and went on to say that I had recently been spending time investigating clouds and the fact that they have names. And it would seem even going as far as having a wide range of functions. So, he said to me, 'that was a good line of study, what exactly have you found out about clouds that you feel you want me to know about?'. I had another sip of my herbal tea and then went on to say 'clouds are amazing things', I have discovered that there are books and sciences on them, my brother sat quietly, while I gave my account.

I started by saying that clouds are nothing more than water particles, or ice crystals that float around in the atmosphere, a category of ten clouds were listed in the Eighteenth Century. This was the work of an Englishmen who was a pharmacist by profession but had written papers on clouds and their formations, his name is Luke Howard and he used Latin to describe these clouds which I thought led to them having a sort of ring about them. Take for example how he would both name and explain a particular cloud or its formation, when he talked about cloud position he may talk about a high cloud as Alto, conversely when he talked about a cloud's appearance, he would use the word, Stratus.

Suffice to say I didn't dwell on the finer technicalities of the science of clouds; I was keen to explain to my brother the spiritual element of clouds if one can think of clouds as having spiritual content. I went on to tell my brother that over many years, I had been taken by the notion that people and their respective clouds could be put, as it were, into categories. My brother's eyes seemed to light up at the point of hearing me say that, he asked me to give him an example of where one can derive spiritual content that people have from clouds. This question immediately brought me back to the Headmaster's office all those years ago, the sad end to what I have to say has remained etched in my mind as being one of the finest sexual encounters I had to date.

I was indeed in the process of telling my brother what I had discovered all those years ago. I remember saying that although I had a fluffy white cloud myself at the time of being in the Headmaster's office; and my cloud did not react in the same way as the other two people in the room. This to me, was the first indication that cloud behaviour could be affected by the intentions of the person that the cloud belonged to. The moment Neola Marton was asked if I had been taking advantage of her, I remember she lowered her head and started to cry, at no point did she ever say that she was a consenting party. It was at this moment I remembered that Neola Marton's cloud started to merge with the Headmaster's; it was as though they had become one.

Though my cloud was still very much fluffy and white, I felt as if the spirit within me did not allow my cloud to merge with Neola Marton's or the Headmaster's. That turned out to be the first occasion on a personal level that I had witnessed clouds merge. Then the second was the time Fod, Hooly and I witnessed the beating of the guy at the river bank also all those years ago. Again, that was a time when it was clear that clouds and people can be placed, it would seem, into categories. It was much later that I told my brother that I realised the spirit of a person can be; it seemed linked to the type of cloud they had. I went on to say that, on more occasions than not, it seemed that people who sported fluffy white clouds could operate on a very clinical or, what I might describe as being, a cold level, and yet it did not seem that way from a distance.

Conversely, I went on to say that on more occasions than not, people sporting pristine shimmering black clouds, merged in the same way as those who sported fluffy white clouds. But there always seemed to be a very clear and fundamental difference in the spirit of those sporting pristine shimmering black clouds. My brother asked if I would like another slice of mum's special cake, and I must confess by now the full effects of that most fantastic cake had well and truly taken effect. I replied at once by saying 'is my cloud black?', to which my brother let out a mighty roar of laughter, followed by him sliding another healthy slice of cake onto my plate.

Take the phrase Altostratus; this would be describing both the height and appearance of a cloud, for example. But in my story about a cloud, I have focussed on two or three clouds out of a category of ten, this I must point out does not mean that I found other clouds uninteresting, but human clouds had only three permanent states. pristine shimmering black, fluffy white and transparent, there are indeed other variations of colour in between the pristine shimmering black clouds and the fluffy white clouds. I related to my brother that there seemed to be a trend that people would use when describing atmospheric clouds. I said I noticed that people would often associate cloud colour and formations with human moods.

This was something I found particularly interesting because it seemed to suggest that not only were our moods governed by those ideas, but so was our perception of colour. This, I think, was a primary factor in me wanting to find out if indeed, these factors were what we use to describe human clouds. It seemed that my memory of human clouds did not follow that theme, I think back to when I too used to sport a great fluffy white cloud. I remember being very happy any time I would look up at it, this as you would remember lasted right up until that fateful day when Neola Marton and myself were summoned to the Headmaster's office, this was indeed the beginning of the change in my cloud's colouration. I realise that I have missed out on a very important point, and that point is that it is thought that all humans are issued with a pristine shimmering black cloud from the moment the sperm reaches the egg. But from that moment onwards, the colour of your cloud at birth can be directly related to the type of information that had been fed to you while in the womb.

At this point, my brother looked at me in utter surprise; he exclaimed you have been doing your homework. I replied by saying it's very difficult to put forward a case on any subject, without having as wide a knowledge as one can have. So, my brother returned my focus to the idea of whether people would use the same form of judgments that are often attributed to atmospheric clouds. All the while, my brother had very strong opinions on this very point. But my brother was keen to hear my opinion, so he led me by reminding me of the story I had told him about the steel toe-capped wearing gang all those years ago. He went on to say, I want you to analyse using the example you have given to me relating to how people define atmospheric clouds, to what you had witnessed all those years ago. I paused as I thought this to be a very important question; I felt that I wanted to give such a question full justice and merit. I thought back to when I was much younger, and the very day I had come across the steel toe-capped wearing gang. Though as I mentioned earlier, it was true that all the members of that gang were sporting fluffy white clouds, I must remind you of the fact that they did not all share the same racial background. You take, for instance, the one called Bruiser; he, in fact, was the leader of this gang and did not share the same racial background as the ones he was leading.

I can confirm that he shared the same racial grouping as me, but in no way will I claim to have any other attributes there from. I started by saying I had never seen a group of people sporting pristine shimmering black clouds, ever set about on anybody. The most I can ever remember about such groups was either a combination of something spiritual, musical, artistic and/or inventive. That does not mean by any stretch that people who sport pristine shimmering black clouds do not have confrontation, but their confrontation often seems to be steeped with the idea of restoring justice where justice is absent. This, therefore, could not in my humble opinion be said about groups that sported fluffy white clouds, these groups would often amass and the larger the group became, the more there seemed to be a temptation to act unjustly.

A few instances come to mind, for example, the events in the Headmaster's office, the story of the older brother of the guy who wore the red, yellow and green hat and finally the steel toe-capped wearing gang. Now the question arises which of the categorisations has the most merit and indeed why?

At this very moment, the name Malcom Little came to mind. Many of us know him as Malcom X. Malcom talked about a time when he was incarcerated and was given a lesson by another inmate. He was asked to take out a dictionary and look up the definition of the word black, then to do the same with the word white.

I must confess to say that if you indeed have a spare moment, this is a wonderful way to gain a sense of what the most common views on the colours black and white might mean. Once knowing these definitions, it becomes important to see if they make sense within your own lives, and whether or not one feels that an adjustment is needed in order to have a balanced view. Alas, I hear and feel your utter confusion, along with the idea that everything you previously understood is about to be turned on its head. Now that you have, in fact, carried out the same lesson as Malcom X, I shall not list the definitions that are to be found in the clear majority of so-called concise dictionaries.

But herein lies my very point of contention, in the news, mass media, and literature, there seems to be a concerted effort in mirroring the definitions of colour in the same way as can be found in the dictionaries of the day. This idea went against everything I had come to understand about colour, though I confess that my understanding of colour came directly from my experience of human clouds. I could at this point go as far as saying that my experience of colour, and/or the interpretation of colour is at complete odds with that which can be found nestled in the pages of the concise dictionaries. My experience showed me that the total opposite could be said of the colours black and white.

Take, for example, the account of the guy who sported a red, yellow and green hat, his entire family sported fluffy white clouds, he was the only member of his family that did not. He remembered feeling like a total stranger in the house he grew up in and would often find most comfort and peace in the company of his neighbour, who incidentally had the same cloud colouration as him but did not share the same racial background. I remember when he gave his account of how his own family would meet up with friends, and before the night was out there would be the formation of a super fluffy white cloud, which he said would always be followed by aggressive language, violent posturing and a frenzied-like mob intent on creating personal harm to specific members of the community. Though he said that the clear majority of the meetings held at his childhood home did not end up with some members of the community being set upon, he said that he was certain that a sizeable number of violent attacks had definitely resulted from such meetings.

This view seemed to tie in with the views I had come to observe on my journey to understanding the perception that society places on colour. In contrast, the guy who sported the red, yellow and green hat would talk about just how peaceful and tranquil it was to be in the company of those that sported shimmering pristine black clouds. He talked about feelings of spirituality, justice and love, a total contrast to what he would be exposed to within his childhood home. I thought at length, how could there be such a vast difference between the concise dictionaries' version of colour, and what I had been exposed to in my life's journey? For me, it seemed like for every negative connotation the word black would contain, I seemed to be able to find the positive. For example, take the Black Hole, for some simply a dark mass in the sky, for others it is the greatest source of power known to man simply because no light can escape it.

Or the word black being associated with abject gloom, then I look at all the Judges with their long black robes, and I see the pinnacle of power. Or even the word black being sinister, I then think of all the years we would be taught in schools by the power of the blackboard. Therein lies a series of so-called negatives, that with a little closer inspection denotes a range of positives. There, of course, comes a time in which one can do the same with the word white for example. So, in the spirit of things, I shall attempt to do the same with the word white, strangely do I notice a moment of slight agitation on your part? I sense a defensive posture has come about?

Take, for example, the word white. Phrases like pure come to mind or clean, but immediately I see the words cold and stark, or the word good is often used to describe the colour white, but I see the words Ku Klux Klan in white from head to toe. White is often associated with brightness, or light, for me the words blinding, or fragile come straight to mind. This then is a book about clouds, but as previously mentioned, no ordinary clouds, the clouds we are given at birth are not fixed in stone, and each and every one of us can have/make a choice on what type and colour of cloud we have. Our social conditioning will impact that choice, but with an eagerness for a just and rewarding life, I am confident that man will see that downside is up and upside is down.

I trust then that you have indeed found patience with me, in reaching this point in my story about a cloud. By now, I am sure you realise that, in fact, my story about a cloud can be more related to perception, and the way in which we choose to see our lives. My cloud has changed as my perceptions have also changed; these changes have been fundamental to my personal development. Having in my opinion, being given the gift of having more than one cloud, has opened my life to experiences that would otherwise have been missed. It also allowed me to have an informed opinion on a variety of topics such as, culture, race, spirituality, love, deception, betrayal, brutality, law, and justice, this list has not been exhausted. I also mentioned that some of you may indeed have a cloud in your own life, and for others, this may be a totally new phenomenon. I therefore, turn the last three questions, in turn, over to thee:

Is it just a cloud?

Is it just a choice?

Is it just a social condition?

THE END

Printed in Great Britain
by Amazon